THE WORSHIP SCROLL

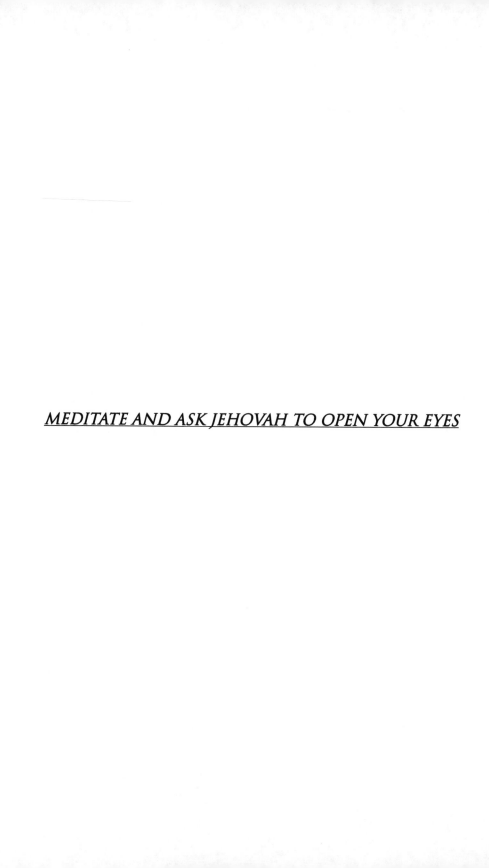

MEDITATE AND ASK JEHOVAH TO OPEN YOUR EYES

THE WORSHIP SCROLL

I AM ELIJAH WHO HAS COME

VERNON SKINNER

authorHOUSE®

AuthorHouse™
1663 Liberty Drive
Bloomington, IN 47403
www.authorhouse.com
Phone: 1-800-839-8640

First published by AuthorHouse   01/24/2012

ISBN: 978-1-4670-4243-7 (sc)
ISBN: 978-1-4670-4242-0 (ebk)

Printed in the United States of America

JEWS AND CHRISTIANS MUST UNITE

ROOT AND BRANCHES

IS

THE BODY OF CHRIST

KNOW THAT

LIGHT OVERCOMES DARKNESS

TABLE OF CONTENTS

MEDITATE AND ASK JEHOVAH TO OPEN YOUR EYES

JEHOVAH'S LAW LIVING AND WORKING IN ME.

WHEN I WAS TOLD TO WRITE THIS BOOK,
BY THE HOLY SPIRIT,
I QUESTIONED WHETHER IT WAS MY HUMAN
MIND
PLAYING TRICKS ON ME OR JEHOVAH.

BUT, WHEN I CONTINUED TO ASK GOD TO REVEAL
HIMSELF
TO ME IN DIFFERENT WAYS AND, HE DID.
I HAD TO BELIEVE JEHOVAH WAS REALLY SPEAKING
TO ME.
MY SITUATION REMINDED ME ABOUT PAUL IN,

ROMANS 7.

PAUL SAID,

"I DO NOT UNDERSTAND WHAT I DO. FOR WHAT
I WANT TO DO I DO NOT DO, BUT WHAT I HATE I
DO. AND IF I DO WHAT I DO NOT WANT

TO DO, I AGREE THAT THE LAW IS GOOD. AS IT IS,
IT IS NO LONGER I MYSELF WHO DO IT, BUT IT IS
SIN LIVING IN ME. I KNOW THAT

NOTHING GOOD LIVES IN ME, THAT IS, IN MY
SINFUL NATURE. FOR I HAVE THE DESIRE TO DO
WHAT IS GOOD, BUT I CANNOT CARRY IT OUT.

1

FOR WHAT I DO IS NOT THE GOOD I WANT TO DO; NO, THE EVIL I DO NOT WANT TO DO—THIS I KEEP ON DOING. NOW IF I DO WHAT I

DO NOT WANT TO DO, IT IS NO LONGER I WHO DO IT, BUT IT IS SIN LIVING IN ME THAT DOES IT.

SO I FIND THIS LAW AT WORK: WHEN I WANT TO DO GOOD, EVIL IS RIGHT THERE WITH ME. FOR IN MY INNER BEING I DELIGHT IN GOD'S LAW; BUT I SEE ANOTHER LAW AT WORK IN THE MEMBERS OF MY BODY, WAGING WAR AGAINST THE LAW OF MY MIND AND MAKING ME A PRISONER OF THE LAW OF SIN AT WORK WITHIN MY MEMBERS. WHAT A WRETCHED MAN I AM! WHO WILL RESCUE ME FROM THIS BODY OF DEATH? THANKS BE TO GOD—THROUGH JESUS CHRIST OUR LORD!

SO THEN, I MYSELF IN MY MIND AM A SLAVE TO GOD'S LAW, BUT IN THE SINFUL NATURE A SLAVE TO THE LAW OF SIN."

THIS BOOK WAS WRITTEN BY JESUS CHRIST IN ME.

FORWARD BY JOANNE JOHNSON

OUR FAMILY MET VERNON BACK IN 2003 WHEN OUR TEENAGE CHILD WAS AT A RESIDENTIAL TREATMENT CENTER FOR CHILDREN WITH

MENTAL ILLNESS.VERNON WAS OUR CHILD'S THERAPIST AND WAS THE "BEST OF THE BEST" IN THE FIELD. NOT ONLY WAS VERNON

GREAT AT HIS PROFESSION, HE WAS A RESPECTFUL, LOVING, CARING HUMAN BEING AND ONE OF THE MOST BEAUTIFUL SOULS YOU WILL

EVER MEET IN YOUR LIFETIME! VERNON ADDED A VERY IMPORTANT ELEMENT IN HELPING OUR FAMILY; THIS WAS HIS INTENSE BELIEF

IN GOD AND HIS SPIRITUALITY (AND I WAS THE ONLY RELIGIOUS ONE IN OUR FAMILY). VERNON IS THE REAL THING AND AS A RESULT

OF OUR CONNECTION WITH HIM, OUR FAMILY HAVE BEEN BROUGHT TOGETHER AS A STRONG FAMILY UNIT, IN-SPITE OF THE RAPTORS OF

MENTAL ILLNESS! WE STILL STRUGGLE FROM TIME TO TIME, BUT WE KNOW HOW TO COPE AND REMAIN A LOVING FAMILY BECAUSE WE

WERE TOUCHED BY VERNON'S BEAUTIFUL SOUL AND GODLY PRESENCE! SOMETIMES IN LIFE YOU MEET AN AMAZING PERSON WHO

BECOMES A PART OF YOUR HEART FOREVER! OUR FAMILY WAS LUCKY ENOUGH (BY THE GRACE OF GOD) TO HAVE VERNON CROSS OUR

PATH IN OUR LIFE JOURNEY, AND WE WILL FOREVER BE INDEBTED TO HIM!

MICROBIOLOGIST SPECIALIST AT MERCK
NAMI TEACHER AND VOLUNTEER

MEDITATE AND ASK JEHOVAH TO OPEN YOUR EYES

ELIJAH MUST COME FIRST AND RESTORE ALL THINGS BEFORE JESUS RETURNS

MALACHI 4:1-6

THE DAY OF THE LORD

"SURELY THE DAY IS COMING; IT WILL BURN LIKE A
FURNACE.
ALL THE ARROGANT AND EVERY EVILDOER WILL
BE STUBBLE,
AND THAT DAY THAT IS COMING WILL SET THEM
ON FIRE," SAYS THE LORD ALMIGHTY.
"NOT A ROOT OR A BRANCH WILL BE LEFT TO
THEM.
BUT FOR YOU WHO REVERE MY NAME,
JEHOVAH
THE SUN OF RIGHTEOUSNESS(JESUS) WILL RISE
WITH HEALING IN ITS WINGS.
AND YOU WILL GO OUT AND LEAP LIKE CALVES
RELEASED FROM THE STALL.
THEN YOU WILL TRAMPLE DOWN THE WICKED;
THEY WILL BE ASHES UNDER THE SOLES OF YOUR
FEET ON THE DAY WHEN I DO THESE THINGS,"
SAYS THE LORD ALMIGHTY.
"REMEMBER THE LAW OF MY SERVANT MOSES,
(THE TEN COMMANDMENTS IS STILL IMPORTANT)
THE DECREES AND LAWS I GAVE HIM AT HOREB
FOR ALL ISRAEL.

"SEE,
I WILL SEND YOU THE PROPHET ELIJAH BEFORE
THAT GREAT AND DREADFUL DAY OF THE LORD
COMES.
HE WILL TURN THE HEARTS OF THE FATHERS TO
THEIR CHILDREN,
—WE HAVE TO LOVE EACHOTHER, JEWS AND
GENTILES—
AND THE HEARTS OF THE CHILDREN TO THEIR
FATHERS;
OR ELSE
I, JEHOVAH, WILL COME AND STRIKE THE LAND
WITH A CURSE."

IF WE DON'T LOVE EACHOTHER;
I MEAN ALL THE PEOPLE WHO PROFESS TO LOVE
JESUS CHRIST,
WE WILL BE DOOMED.

ELIJAH, THE NAME THE HOLY SPIRIT GAVE ME

I, ELIJAH, THE NAME THE HOLY SPIRIT GAVE ME ON 06/21/11. THE HOLY SPIRIT SAID TO ME, "YOU ARE ELIJAH WHO HAS COME." I GIVE ALL HONOR, THANKS, PRAISE AND GLORY TO JEHOVAH, MY LORD AND SAVIOR JESUS CHRIST AND THE HOLY SPIRIT. MY GOD AND LORD HAS ANOINTED ME AND GIVEN ME A WONDERFUL TASK TO UNITE THE WORLD THROUGH LOVE OF JEHOVAH AND, PRAISE AND WORSHIP BEFORE HIS NEXT COMING, THE GREAT DAY OF THE LORD. I KNOW THE ELECT HAS ALREADY STARTED TO UNITE IN ITS OWN NATURAL SPIRITUAL WAY BUT, WHAT MAKES ME DIFFERENT IS, GOD ACTUALLY HAS GIVEN ME ACCESS TO HIS GENERAL PLANS. IF SOMEONE ELSE CLAIMED THEY HAD A PLAN, I COULD NOT DISPUTE IT BUT, GOD JEHOVAH CAN. I OBEY MY GOD.

GOD'S PLAN MOST BASIC ELEMENT HAS TO DO WITH FOCUSING ON CHANGING HOW MOST OF THE ELECT LOVE EACH OTHER, RESPECT THE AUTHORITY OF THE CHURCH AND THE AUTHORITY IN THE CHURCH, WORSHIP HIM AND BRINGING CHRIST'S BODY INTO COMPLETE UNITY. GOD WANTS THE WHOLE FOCUS OF OUR LOVE AND WORSHIP TO BE AROUND WHAT HE COMMANDED US TO DO. GOD WANTS MORE OF CORINTHIANS 13 TYPE OF LOVE THAN ANY OTHER LOVE CREATED BY MAN. IN REGARDS TO WORSHIP, GOD WANTS

US TO SPEND MORE TIME WITH HIM, FOCUSING ON HIM. THE HOLY SPIRIT TOLD ME, "WHEN YOU FOCUS ON ME, I FOCUS ON YOU. IN YOUR WORSHIP SONGS, THE MUSIC IS MINE AND THE WORDS ARE YOURS. PRAISE ME ALONE."

THE WORSHIP SCROLL IS PART OF GOD'S PLAN TO UNITE HIS PEOPLE, THE CALLED, AROUND THE WORLD. THE WORSHIP SCROLL IS DESIGNED BY THE HOLY SPIRIT TO ALLOW US TO GIVE GOD MORE SPECIFIC AND PRODUCTIVE TIME WORSHIPING HIM. THE WORSHIP SCROLL HELP US CLEAN AND RENEW OUR MINDS IN A DISCIPLINE AND STRUCTURED WAY BECAUSE, THE HOLY SPIRIT HIMSELF WILL COME AND HELP US THROUGH THE CLEANING AND LEARNING PROCESS.

BEFORE WORSHIPING AND MEDITATING ON THE WORSHIP SCROLL, INDIVIDUALS SHOULD FIRST REPENT AND SAY THE LORD'S PRAYER. THE IDEAL GOAL OF THE WORSHIPER IS TO WORSHIP AND MEDITATE ON EACH LINE OF THE, 1000 LINE, WORSHIP SCROLL FOR ONE MINUTER OR MORE. MOST OF US MAY NOT BE ABLE TO ACCOMPLISH 1000 LINES AT ONE MINUTE WORSHIP EACH LINE THE FIRST TIME AROUND. THEREFORE, INDIVIDUALS SHOULD PRACTICE SHORTER TIME FRAMES PER LINE TO BEGIN WITH. AS YOU PRACTICE AND USE THE WORSHIP SCROLL, HAVE A NOTEBOOK AND START DOCUMENTING YOUR INTERNAL AND EXTERNAL MESSAGES, ESPECIALLY YOUR DREAMS. AT TIMES FIND A WIDE OPEN PEACEFUL FIELD TO WORSHIP ALONE OR WITH OTHER WORSHIPERS. ALSO, AS PART OF YOUR LEARNING PROCESS, REPENT DAILY AND PURIFY YOURSELF OF ALL NEGATIVE THOUGHTS AND ACTIONS. READING CORINTHIANS 13 AND MEDITATING ON IT DAILY WILL ALSO ADD TO YOUR SPIRITUAL STRENGTH AND INCREASE YOUR LEVEL

OF CONNECTIVITY WITH THE HOLY SPIRIT. WE SHOULD FOCUS ON LOVE'S MAIN CHARACTERISTICS; LOVE IS PATIENT, LOVE IS KIND, IT DOES NOT BOAST, IT IS NOT PROUD, IT DOES NOT DISHONOR OTHERS, IT IS NOT SELF-SEEKING, IT IS NOT EASILY ANGERED, IT KEEPS NO RECORD OF WRONGS, LOVE DOES NOT DELIGHT IN EVIL, LOVE REJOICES WITH THE TRUTH, LOVE ALWAYS PROTECTS, LOVE ALWAYS TRUSTS, LOVE ALWAYS HOPES, LOVE ALWAYS PERSEVERES AND LOVE NEVER FAILS.

WE MUST ALWAYS REMEMBER, LOVE BELONGS TO GOD. AS THE FOLLOWING BIBLE CHAPTER AND VERSES MENTIONED; 1 JOHN 4:8, "WHOEVER DOES NOT LOVE DOES NOT KNOW GOD, BECAUSE GOD IS LOVE." 1 JOHN 4:20, "IF ANYONE SAYS, "I LOVE GOD," YET HATES HIS BROTHER, HE IS A LIAR. FOR ANYONE WHO DOES NOT LOVE HIS BROTHER, WHOM HE HAS SEEN, CANNOT LOVE GOD, WHOM HE HAS NOT SEEN." DEUTERONOMY 7:9,"KNOW THEREFORE THAT THE LORD YOUR GOD IS GOD; HE IS THE FAITHFUL GOD, KEEPING HIS COVENANT OF LOVE TO A THOUSAND GENERATIONS OF THOSE WHO LOVE HIM AND KEEP HIS COMMANDS." 1 CORINTHIANS 8:3, "BUT THE MAN WHO LOVES GOD IS KNOWN BY GOD." JAMES 1:12, "BLESSED IS THE MAN WHO PERSEVERES UNDER TRIAL, BECAUSE WHEN HE HAS STOOD THE TEST, HE WILL RECEIVE THE CROWN OF LIFE THAT GOD HAS PROMISED TO THOSE WHO LOVE HIM." 1 JOHN 4:9, "THIS IS HOW GOD SHOWED HIS LOVE AMONG US: HE SENT HIS ONE AND ONLY SON INTO THE WORLD THAT WE MIGHT LIVE THROUGH HIM." 1 JOHN 4:10, "THIS IS LOVE: NOT THAT WE LOVED GOD, BUT THAT HE LOVED US AND SENT HIS SON AS AN ATONING SACRIFICE FOR OUR SINS." 1 JOHN 4:12, "NO ONE HAS EVER SEEN GOD; BUT IF WE LOVE ONE ANOTHER, GOD LIVES IN US AND HIS LOVE IS MADE COMPLETE IN US." 1 JOHN

4:16, "AND SO WE KNOW AND RELY ON THE LOVE GOD HAS FOR US. GOD IS LOVE. WHOEVER LIVES IN LOVE LIVES IN GOD, AND GOD IN HIM." 1 JOHN 5:1, "EVERYONE WHO BELIEVES THAT JESUS IS THE CHRIST IS BORN OF GOD, AND EVERYONE WHO LOVES THE FATHER LOVES HIS CHILD AS WELL." 1 JOHN 5:2, "THIS IS HOW WE KNOW THAT WE LOVE THE CHILDREN OF GOD: BY LOVING GOD AND CARRYING OUT HIS COMMANDS." 1 JOHN 5:3, "THIS IS LOVE FOR GOD: TO OBEY HIS COMMANDS. AND HIS COMMANDS ARE NOT BURDENSOME . . ."

IT IS MY PERSONAL PRAYER FOR YOU, THAT JEHOVAH WILL DO EXACTLY WHAT HE TOLD ME HE WILL DO FOR YOU, WHEN YOU MEDITATE ON HIS WORSHIP SCROLL DAILY; THE HOLY SPIRIT WILL COME AND LOVE AND ENLIGHTENING YOU WHILE CREATING MIRACLES IN YOUR LIFE.

IN JESUS CHRIST NAME, AMEN

MEDITATE AND ASK JEHOVAH TO OPEN YOUR EYES

WORSHIP KEYS

INTIMACY WITH GOD)

KEEP FOCUS ON GOD

PARTICIPATE IN ALL WORSHIP

DO NOT AT ANYTIME THINK ABOUT YOUR SELF

DO NOT CUT YOUR WORSHIP OFF TO SOON

LET YOUR WORSHIP FLOW

DO NOT THINK ABOUT TIME

DO NOT FOCUS ON YOUR PAIN, GOD KNOWS

FOCUS ON GOD'S LOVE

FOCUS ON GOD'S POWER

FOCUS ON THE BLOOD OF JESUS

PRAISE GOD FOR BEING A GREAT FATHER

PRAISE FOR OVER ONE HOUR OR MORE DAILY

PRACTICE THE PRESENCE OF JESUS WITH YOUR
BODY

NEVER SEE WORSHIP AS BORING

DO NOT EVOKE THE FLESH

GOD IS IN YOUR MOUTH AND HE WANTS TO
COME OUT

ENCOURAGE YOUR FAMILY AND FRIENDS TO
WORSHIP LOUDLY

WHAT YOU SOW YOU SHALL REEP

WORSHIP WORDS: FATHER, JESUS, LORD, GOD,
HEAVEN, EARTH, PRAISE, HOLY, THANKS, GREAT,
ALMIGHTY, SING, GOOD, ROCK, WORTHY, LOVE,
PLEASANT, EXTOL,
MIGHTY, EXALT, GLORY, HEALER, PEACE, KIND,
MERCY, MERCIFUL
GOD INHALES YOUR WORSHIP AND EXHALES HIS
GLORY

MEDITATE AND ASK JEHOVAH TO OPEN YOUR EYES

CALL SIGN

THE WORSHIP SCROLL IS JEHOVAH'S-:
WORSHIP SCROLL—OF A 1000 LINES

HAVE YOU EVER WONDERED WHY THE ANGELS
WORSHIP JESUS LIKE THEY DO.

GOD HAS GIVEN US THE WORSHIP SCROLL TO
FIND OUT.
HUNGER AND THURST FOR JESUS,
WORSHIP LIKE THE ANGELS IN REVELATIONS

SEEK AND FIND JESUS LOVE THROUGH LOVING
OTHERS
"REPENT AND PRAY (ALOUD) THE LORD'S PRAYER
BEFORE WORSHIP"

YOUR GOAL IS TO CONSISTANTLY GIVE JEHOVAH
MORE OF YOUR TIME DAILY

17 HOURS PRAISE AND WORSHIP—ONE MINUTE
PER LINE

OUR CONNECTION TO GOD IS VOICE ACTIVATED

AND

WHAT WE SAY MATTERS MORE THAN YOU THINK.

MEDITATE AND ASK JEHOVAH TO OPEN YOUR EYES

GOD'S BLESSINGS ARE VOICE ACTIVATED.

AS YOU START THE WORSHIP SCROLL

REPENT NOW

ASKING JEHOVAH FOR MERCY
AND PROMISE TO GIVE MERCY
TO ALL

NOW COMPLETE THE
LORD'S PRAYER

MEDITATE ON EACH LINE OF THE PRAYER

"FATHER JEHOVAH GOD,

HALLOWED(HOLY, SANCTIFIED) BE YOUR NAME,. . . .
YOUR KINGDOM COME, ...
GIVE US, ...
EACH DAY, ...
OUR DAILY BREAD, ...
FORGIVE US, ...
OUR SINS, ...
FOR WE ALSO, ...
FORGIVE EVERYONE, ...
WHO SINS AGAINST US, ...
AND LEAD US, ...
NOT INTO TEMPTATION," . . . .
AND DELIVER US FROM THE EVIL ONE . . . .

FOR THINE IS THE KINGDOM . . . .
THE POWER AND THE GLORY . . . .
FOREVER AND EVER . . . .
AMEN . . . .

MEDITATE AND ASK JEHOVAH TO OPEN YOUR EYES

PSALM 26:6-7

SCRIPTURE
GOD'S WORSHIP SCROLL:-<u>CALL SIGN</u>
PSALM 26:6-7

WASH MY HANDS IN INNOCENCE,
AND GO ABOUT YOUR ALTAR, O LORD,
PROCLAIMING ALOUD YOUR PRAISE
AND TELLING OF ALL YOUR WONDERFUL DEEDS.

NOW START THE
JESUS WORSHIP SCROLL

1. GOD JESUS YOU SAID BLESSED IS HE WHO COMES IN THE NAME OF THE LORD, I WORSHIP YOU LORD JESUS, I PRAISE YOU LORD, HALLELUJAH.
2. I KNOW YOU ARE A SPIRIT LORD AND I WILL WORSHIP YOU IN SPIRIT AND IN TRUTH, HALLELUJAH, I PRAISE YOU GOD JESUS.
3. MY LORD JESUS YOU ARE THE PRINCE OF PEACE, I PRAISE YOU LORD AND MY GOD JESUS, HALLELUJAH.
4. IN YOUR PRESENCE I GIVE ALL CONTROL LORD JESUS, I PRAISE YOU JESUS, HALLELUJAH
5. I WILL STRETCH MY TIME WITH YOU LORD JESUS, I PRAISE YOU JESUS, HALLELUJAH.
6. I WILL STRETCH MY GIFTS AND UNDEFILED OFFERINGS TO YOU JESUS, BECAUSE YOU LOVE ME, I PRAISE YOU LORD JESUS, HALLELUJAH.
7. GOD JESUS YOU SAID BLESSED ARE THE POOR IN SPIRIT, FOR THEIRS IS THE KINGDOM OF HEAVEN, I PRAISE YOU LORD JESUS, HALLELUJAH.
8. GOD JESUS YOU SAID BLESSED ARE THOSE WHO MOURN, FOR THEY WILL BE COMFORTED, I PRAISE YOU LORD JESUS, HALLELUJAH.

9. GOD JESUS YOU SAID BLESSED ARE THE MEEK, FOR THEY WILL INHERIT THE EARTH, I PRAISE YOU JESUS, HALLELUJAH.

10. GOD JESUS YOU SAID BLESSED ARE THOSE WHO HUNGER AND THIRST FOR RIGHTEOUSNESS, FOR THEY WILL BE FILLED, I PRAISE YOU JESUS, HALLELUJAH.

11. GOD JESUS YOU SAID BLESSED ARE THE MERCIFUL, FOR THEY WILL BE SHOWN MERCY, I PRAISE YOU JESUS, HALLELUJAH.

12. GOD JESUS YOU SAID BLESSED ARE THE PURE IN HEART, FOR THEY WILL SEE GOD, I PRAISE YOU JESUS, HALLELUJAH.

13. GOD JESUS YOU SAID BLESSED ARE THE PEACEMAKERS, FOR THEY WILL BE CALLED SONS OF GOD, I PRAISE YOU JESUS, HALLELUJAH.

14. GOD JESUS YOU SAID BLESSED ARE THOSE WHO ARE PERSECUTED BECAUSE OF RIGHTEOUSNESS, FOR THEIRS IS THE KINGDOM OF HEAVEN, I PRAISE YOU JESUS, HALLELUJAH.

15. GOD JESUS YOU SAID BLESSED ARE YOU WHEN PEOPLE INSULT YOU, PERSECUTE YOU AND FALSELY SAY ALL KINDS OF EVIL AGAINST YOU BECAUSE OF ME, I PRAISE YOU JESUS, HALLELUJAH.

16. GOD JESUS YOU SAID REJOICE AND BE GLAD, BECAUSE GREAT IS MY REWARD IN HEAVEN, I PRAISE YOU JESUS, HALLELUJAH.

17. I BELIEVE IN THE SON OF THE LIVING GOD ADONAI, I PRAISE YOU JESUS, HALLELUJAH.

18. HOSANNA IN THE HIGHEST! I PRAISE YOU JESUS, HALLELUJAH.

19. HOSANNA IN THE HIGHEST! BLESSED IS HE WHO COMES IN THE NAME OF THE LORD!" I PRAISE YOU JESUS, HALLELUJAH.

20. HOSANNA TO THE SON OF DAVID, I PRAISE YOU JESUS, HALLELUJAH.

21. HOSANNA IN THE HIGHEST! I PRAISE YOU JESUS, HALLELUJAH.
22. HOSANNA IN THE HIGHEST! BLESSED IS HE WHO COMES IN THE NAME OF THE LORD! I PRAISE YOU JESUS, HALLELUJAH.
23. HOSANNA TO THE SON OF DAVID. I PRAISE YOU JESUS, HALLELUJAH.
24. GREAT IS YOUR MERCY LORD, I PRAISE YOU JESUS, HALLELUJAH.
25. HOLY HOLY HOLY IS THE LORD GOD ALMIGHTY JESUS CHRIST, I PRAISE YOU JESUS.
26. HOLY HOLY HOLY IS THE LORD GOD ALMIGHTY JESUS CHRIST, I PRAISE YOU JESUS.
27. HOLY HOLY HOLY IS THE LORD GOD ALMIGHTY JESUS CHRIST, I PRAISE YOU JESUS.
28. HOLY HOLY HOLY IS THE LORD GOD ALMIGHTY JESUS CHRIST, I PRAISE YOU JESUS.
29. HOLY HOLY HOLY IS THE LORD GOD ALMIGHTY JESUS CHRIST, I PRAISE YOU JESUS.
30. HOLY HOLY HOLY IS THE LORD GOD ALMIGHTY JESUS CHRIST, I PRAISE YOU JESUS.
31. HOLY HOLY HOLY IS THE LORD GOD ALMIGHTY JESUS CHRIST, I PRAISE YOU JESUS.
32. HALLELUJAH, HALLELUJAH, HALLELUJAH, I PRAISE YOU JESUS.
33. HALLELUJAH, HALLELUJAH, HALLELUJAH, I PRAISE YOU JESUS.
34. HALLELUJAH, HALLELUJAH, HALLELUJAH, I PRAISE YOU JESUS.
35. HALLELUJAH, HALLELUJAH, HALLELUJAH, I PRAISE YOU JESUS.
36. HALLELUJAH, HALLELUJAH, HALLELUJAH, I PRAISE YOU JESUS.
37. HALLELUJAH, HALLELUJAH, HALLELUJAH, I PRAISE YOU JESUS.
38. HAVE MERCY ON ME JESUS FOR I SIN AGAINST YOU, I PRAISE YOU, HALLELUJAH.

39. HAVE MERCY ON ME JESUS FOR I SIN AGAINST YOU, I PRAISE YOU, HALLELUJAH.
40. HAVE MERCY ON ME JESUS FOR I SIN AGAINST YOU, I PRAISE YOU, HALLELUJAH.
41. HALLELUJAH, HALLELUJAH, HALLELUJAH, JESUS.
42. LORD GOD ALMIGHTY JESUS CHRIST, I PRAISE YOU, HALLELUJAH.
43. HALLELUJAH, HALLELUJAH, HALLELUJAH, JESUS.
44. LORD GOD ALMIGHTY JESUS CHRIST, I PRAISE YOU, HALLELUJAH.
45. HALLELUJAH, HALLELUJAH, HALLELUJAH, JESUS.
46. LORD GOD ALMIGHTY JESUS CHRIST, I PRAISE YOU, HALLELUJAH.
47. I PRAISE YOU JESUS, HALLELUJAH.
48. I NEED YOU JESUS, TO SURVIVE, HALLELUJAH.
49. I LOVE YOU JESUS, HALLELUJAH.
50. YOU ARE IMPORTANT TO ME JESUS, HALLELUJAH.
51. COME TO ME JESUS, HALLELUJAH.
52. LET ME FEEL YOU JESUS, HALLELUJAH.
53. I AM HAPPY TO BE PART OF YOUR BODY JESUS, I PRAISE YOU, HALLELUJAH.
54. STAND WITH ME JESUS, HALLELUJAH.
55. YOU ARE GREAT JESUS, HALLELUJAH.
56. YOU ARE HOLY JESUS, HALLELUJAH.
57. YOU ARE FAITHFUL JESUS, HALLELUJAH.
58. JESUS YOU ARE LORD AND GOD, HALLELUJAH.
59. JESUS YOU ARE THE KING OF HEAVEN AND EARTH, I PRAISE YOU, HALLELUJAH.
60. YOU ARE WONDERFUL JESUS, HALLELUJAH.
61. YOU ARE MARVELOUS JESUS, HALLELUJAH.
62. I CALL YOU RIGHTEOUS JESUS, HALLELUJAH.
63. I CALL YOU AWESOME JESUS, HALLELUJAH.
64. YOU ARE WORHTY OF ALL MY PRAISE JESUS, HALLELUJAH.
65. YOU ARE MERCIFUL JESUS, HALLELUJAH.
66. JESUS YOU ARE THE ALPHA AND OMEGA, I PRAISE YOU, HALLELUJAH.

67. YOU ARE THE PEACE MAKER JESUS, HALLELUJAH.
68. YOU ARE THE GLORIOUS JESUS, HALLELUJAH.
69. YOU ARE THE HEALER JESUS, HALLELUJAH.
70. YOU ARE THE LOVING JESUS, HALLELUJAH.
71. YOU ARE THE ROCK JESUS, HALLELUJAH.
72. COME AND HOLD ME JESUS, HALLELUJAH.
73. COME AND LOVE ME JESUS, HALLELUJAH.
74. I CAN'T DO WITHOUT YOU JESUS, HALLELUJAH.
75. SHOW YOURSELF TO ME JESUS, HALLELUJAH.
76. I WORSHIP YOU JESUS, HALLELUJAH.
77. I HONOR YOU JESUS, HALLELUJAH.
78. GREAT IS YOUR MERCY TOWARDS ME JESUS, HALLELUJAH.
79. YOU ARE THE GREAT PROVIDER JESUS, HALLELUJAH.
80. I THANK YOU FOR YOUR KINDNESS JESUS, HALLELUJAH.
81. THANKS FOR BEING MY SAVIOR JESUS, HALLELUJAH.
82. I PRAISE YOUR SPIRIT JESUS, HALLELUJAH.
83. I THANK YOU JESUS FOR GIVING ME ETERNAL LIFE, HALLELUJAH.
84. THANKS FOR BEING JUST TO ME JESUS, HALLELUJAH.
85. I THANK YOU JESUS FOR UNDERSTANDING MY NEEDS, I PRAISE YOU, HALLELUJAH.
86. I PRAISE YOU LORD GOD ALMIGHTY JESUS CHRIST, HALLELUJAH.
87. I PRAISE YOU LORD GOD ALMIGHTY JESUS CHRIST, HALLELUJAH.
88. I PRAISE YOU LORD GOD ALMIGHTY JESUS CHRIST, HALLELUJAH.
89. JESUS YOU ARE WORTHY OF ALL THE GLORY AND THE PRAISE, HALLELUJAH.
90. THERE IS NONE LIKE YOU LORD JESUS, HALLELUJAH.

91. YOU ARE HOLY LORD ALMIGHTY JESUS, HALLELUJAH.
92. YOU ARE HOLY LORD ALMIGHTY JESUS, HALLELUJAH.
93. YOU ARE HOLY LORD ALMIGHTY JESUS, HALLELUJAH.
94. YOU ARE THE LAMB ON THE THRONE JESUS, HALLELUJAH.
95. JESUS YOU ARE THE ONE AND ONLY SON OF GOD THE MOST HIGH, HALLELUJAH.
96. I WANT YOU TO TOUCH ME JESUS, HALLELUJAH.
97. I WANT YOU TO NEVER LEAVE ME JESUS, HALLELUJAH.
98. I WANT YOU ALWAYS IN MY LIFE LORD JESUS, HALLELUJAH.
99. I NEED YOU NOW LORD JESUS, I PRAISE YOU, HALLELUJAH.
100. JESUS YOU ARE THE KING OF KINGS, HALLELUJAH.
101. JESUS YOU ARE THE LORD OF LORDS, HALLELUJAH.
102. JESUS I KNOW YOU LIVE TODAY, I PRAISE YOU, HALLELUJAH.
103. JESUS I KNOW YOU WILL LIVE TOMORROW, I PRAISE YOU JESUS.
104. JESUS THE GOD OF THE BIBLE IS GREAT AND GENEROUS, HALLELUJAH.
105. COME TO ME LORD JESUS LET ME SEE YOU, HALLELUJAH.
106. I WANT YOU TO HOLD ME LORD JESUS, HALLELUJAH.
107. I WANT TO FEEL YOUR LOVE LORD JESUS, HALLELUJAH.
108. JESUS YOU ARE THE CENTER OF MY JOY, I PRAISE YOU, HALLELUJAH.
109. HOLY HOLY HOLY IS THE LORD GOD ALMIGHTY JESUS CHRIST, HALLELUJAH.

110. HOLY HOLY HOLY IS THE LORD GOD ALMIGHTY JESUS CHRIST, HALLELUJAH.
111. HOLY HOLY HOLY IS THE LORD GOD ALMIGHTY JESUS CHRIST, HALLELUJAH.
112. JESUS YOU ARE THE MAJOR PRESENCE IN MY LIFE, HALLELUJAH.
113. JESUS I NEED YOU NOW, HALLELUJAH.
114. JESUS COME RESCUE ME, HALLELUJAH.
115. JESUS DON'T WAIT ONE SECOND BEFORE YOU COME, HALLELUJAH.
116. JESUS I WANT TO SERVE YOU ALONE, HALLELUJAH.
117. HALLELUJAH, HALLELUJAH, HALLELUJAH, JESUS.
118. LORD GOD ALMIGHTY JESUS CHRIST, I PRAISE YOU, HALLELUJAH.
119. HALLELUJAH, HALLELUJAH, HALLELUJAH, JESUS.
120. LORD GOD ALMIGHTY JESUS CHRIST, I PRAISE YOU, HALLELUJAH.
121. HALLELUJAH, HALLELUJAH, HALLELUJAH, JESUS.
122. LORD GOD ALMIGHTY JESUS CHRIST, I PRAISE YOU, HALLELUJAH.
123. I HONOR YOU JESUS, I PRAISE YOU, HALLELUJAH.
124. I WILL CONFORM TO YOUR BLESSED WAYS LORD JESUS, HALLELUJAH.
125. GREAT IS YOUR MERCY MY LORD JESUS, I PRAISE YOU, JESUS.
126. JESUS YOU ARE EVER FAITHFUL, I PRAISE YOU, JESUS.
127. DEAR JESUS YOU ARE THE GREAT I AM, I PRAISE YOU, JESUS.
128. JESUS YOUR TENDER MERCY GIVE US ALL PEACE, I PRAISE YOU JESUS.
129. JESUS YOU ARE THE MIRACLE WORKER, I PRAISE YOU JESUS.

130. JESUS YOU ARE THE HEALER, I PRAISE YOU JESUS.
131. GREAT IS YOUR MERCY LORD, I PRAISE YOU JESUS.
132. JESUS YOU DIED, TO SAVE ME, I WORSHIP YOU LORD JESUS.
133. JESUS YOU DIED, SO I AM HEALED, I WORSHIP YOU LORD JESUS.
134. JESUS YOU DIED, SO I OBTAIN GLORY, I WORSHIP YOU LORD JESUS.
135. JESUS YOU DIED, SO I OBTAIN LIFE, I WORSHIP YOU LORD JESUS.
136. JESUS YOU DIED, TO MAKE ME HAPPY, I WORSHIP YOU LORD JESUS.
137. JESUS YOU DIED, TO GIVE ME HOPE, I WORSHIP YOU LORD JESUS.
138. JESUS YOU DIED, TO GIVE ME YOUR RIGHTEOUSNESS, I WORSHIP YOU LORD JESUS.
139. JESUS YOU DIED, FOR US TO BE TOGETHER, I WORSHIP YOU LORD JESUS.
140. JESUS YOU DIED, TO FREE ME FROM SIN, I WORSHIP YOU LORD JESUS.
141. JESUS YOU DIED, TO GIVE ME ETERNAL LIFE, I WORSHIP YOU LORD JESUS.
142. JESUS YOU DIED, TO PROSPER ME, I WORSHIP YOU LORD JESUS.
143. JESUS YOU DIED, FOR ME TO DEVELOP A RELATIONSHIP WITH YOU, I WORSHIP YOU LORD JESUS.
144. JESUS YOU DIED, FOR ME TO DEVELOP A RELATIONSHIP WITH OUR FATHER GOD, I WORSHIP YOU LORD JESUS.
145. JESUS YOU DIED, FOR ME TO HAVE A RELATIONSHIP WITH THE HOLY SPIRIT, I WORSHIP YOU LORD JESUS.

146. JESUS YOU DIED, TO SHOW ME ALL THE SECRETS OF HEAVEN, I WORSHIP YOU LORD JESUS.
147. JESUS YOU DIED, FOR ME TO KNOW WHAT TRUE LOVE IS, I WORSHIP YOU LORD JESUS.
148. JESUS YOU DIED, SO I KNOW WHAT TRUE OBEDIENCE IS, I WORSHIP YOU LORD JESUS.
149. JESUS I KNOW YOU LIVE TODAY, I PRAISE YOU LORD JESUS.
150. THERE IS NO GOD LIKE YOU JESUS, I PRAISE YOU LORD JESUS.
151. PURIFY ME JESUS, I PRAISE YOU LORD JESUS.
152. MAKE YOURSELF KNOWN TO ME JESUS, I PRAISE YOU LORD JESUS.
153. JESUS YOUR HEART IS CLEAN AND JUST, I PRAISE YOU LORD JESUS.
154. WHEN I CALL YOUR NAME JESUS YOU NEVER SAY NO, I PRAISE YOU LORD JESUS.
155. YOU HAVE PROMISED TO BLESS ME IF I OBEY YOU, I PRAISE YOU LORD JESUS.
156. YOU HAVE PROMISED TO COME NEAR ME IF I COME NEAR YOU, I PRAISE YOU LORD JESUS.
157. YOU HAVE PROMISED TO WATCH OVER AND COUNSEL ME, I PRAISE YOU LORD JESUS.
158. YOU PROMISED NOT A HAIR ON MY HEAD WILL PERISH, I PRAISE YOU LORD JESUS.
159. YOU PROMISED, IF I CALL ON YOU IN TIMES OF TROUBLE; YOU WILL DELIVER ME AND HONOR ME, I PRAISE YOU LORD JESUS.
160. YOU PROMISED TO NEVER FORSAKE ME OR LEAVE ME, I PRAISE YOU LORD JESUS.
161. YOU PROMISED THAT IF I CONFESS MY SINS, YOU WILL BE FAITHFUL AND JUST TO ME, AND YOU WILL FORGIVE ME OF MY SINS AND PURIFY ME FROM ALL UNRIGHTEOUSNESS, I PRAISE YOU LORD JESUS.
162. ONLY YOU ARE HOLY JESUS, I WORSHIP YOU LORD JESUS.

163. ONLY YOU ARE HOLY JESUS, I WORSHIP YOU LORD JESUS.
164. ONLY YOU ARE HOLY JESUS, I WORSHIP YOU LORD JESUS.
165. THE SPIRIT OF GOD IS ON YOU JESUS, I PRAISE YOU LORD JESUS.
166. GOD THE FATHER HAS ANOINTED YOU JESUS, I PRAISE YOU LORD, HALLELUJAH.
167. JESUS YOU PREACHED GOOD NEWS TO THE POOR, I PRAISE YOU LORD, HALLELUJAH.
168. JESUS YOU CAME TO PROCLAIM FREEDOM FOR THE PRISONERS, I PRAISE YOU LORD.
169. RECOVERY OF SIGHT FOR THE BLIND, YOU PROVIDED JESUS, I PRAISE YOU LORD.
170. JESUS, YOU RELEASED THE OPPRESSED, I PRAISE YOU LORD, HALLELUJAH.
171. JESUS YOU PROCLAIM THE YEAR OF THE LORD'S FAVOR, I PRAISE YOU LORD, HALLELUJAH.
172. YOUR GREATEST PLEASURE JESUS IS FOR US TO BELIEVE YOU, I BELIEVE YOU AND WORSHIP YOU LORD JESUS, HALLELUJAH.
173. I DO NOT DOUBT YOU JESUS, I PRAISE YOU LORD, HALLELUJAH.
174. MY LORD JESUS YOU ARE THE GREAT LION OF JUDAH, HALLELUJAH.
175. OH JESUS HOW POWERFUL YOU ARE, I PRAISE YOU, HALLELUJAH.
176. YOU ARE HOLY, LORD JESUS, I PRAISE YOU LORD, HALLELUJAH.
177. YOU ARE HOLY, LORD JESUS, I PRAISE YOU LORD, HALLELUJAH.
178. YOU ARE HOLY, LORD JESUS, I PRAISE YOU GOD, HALLELUJAH.
179. JESUS YOU ARE THE SUN OF MAN, I PRAISE YOU LORD, HALLELUJAH.
180. MY LOVING JESUS BE WITH ME LORD JESUS, I PRAISE YOU, HALLELUJAH.
181. STAY WITH ME LORD JESUS, HALLELUJAH.

182. NEVER LEAVE ME LORD JESUS, HALLELUJAH.
183. I HAVE TO HAVE YOU WITH ME LORD JESUS, HALLELUJAH.
184. I WANT YOU LORD, I PRAISE YOU, HALLELUJAH.
185. I LOVE YOU LORD JESUS, I PRAISE YOU, HALLELUJAH.
186. I WANT YOUR INTENSE LOVE LORD JESUS, HALLELUJAH.
187. SHOW YOURSELF TO ME, LOVING JESUS, HALLELUJAH.
188. YOU MADE THE HEAVENS AND THE EARTH, I WORSHIP YOU JESUS, HALLELUJAH.
189. MY KING IS MY GREATEST POSSESSION, I WORSHIP YOU JESUS, HALLELUJAH.
190. MY REDEEMER FROM EVERLASTING IS YOUR NAME JESUS, HALLELUJAH.
191. YOU ARE AWESOME, YOU ARE AWESOME OUR GOD JESUS, HALLELUJAH.
192. I LOVE YOU JESUS FOREVER, HALLELUJAH.
193. I LIFT MY HANDS UP TO YOU JESUS, I PRAISE YOU, HALLELUJAH.
194. MELODIES FROM HEAVEN RAIN DOWN ON ME, I PRAISE YOU JESUS, HALLELUJAH.
195. GIVE ME ALL YOUR JOY LORD, I PRAISE YOU JESUS, HALLELUJAH.
196. THANKS FOR YOUR PEACE, I WORSHIP YOU JESUS, HALLELUJAH.
197. I THANK YOU FOR THE HOLY SPIRIT, I WORSHIP YOU JESUS, HALLELUJAH.
198. I THANK YOU FOR YOUR BLESSINGS LORD, I WORSHIP YOU JESUS, HALLELUJAH.
199. I THANK YOU FOR GIVING ME UNDERSTANDING LORD, I WORSHIP YOU JESUS, HALLELUJAH.
200. I THANK YOU FOR WISDOM, I WORSHIP YOU JESUS, HALLELUJAH.
201. I THANK YOU FOR LONG LIFE, I WORSHIP YOU JESUS, HALLELUJAH.

202. I THANK YOU FOR GREAT HEALTH, I WORSHIP YOU JESUS, HALLELUJAH.
203. I THANK YOU FOR CHOSING ME FOR SALVATION, I WORSHIP YOU JESUS, HALLELUJAH.
204. YOUR LOVE IS EVERLASTING LORD, I WORSHIP YOU JESUS, HALLELUJAH.
205. NO ONE CAN LOVE ME LIKE YOU LORD, I PRAISE YOU JESUS, HALLELUJAH.
206. NO ONE KNOWS ME LIKE YOU DO, I PRAISE YOU JESUS, HALLELUJAH.
207. YOU ARE ALWAYS IN MY LIFE LORD, I PRAISE YOU JESUS, HALLELUJAH.
208. YOU ARE ALWAYS GIVING ME A LIFE LINE LORD, I PRAISE YOU JESUS, HALLELUJAH.
209. I WILL PRAISE YOU JESUS FOREVER, HALLELUJAH.
210. THE SWORD OF THE SPIRIT COMES FROM YOU JESUS, I PRAISE YOU, HALLELUJAH.
211. JESUS YOU ARE THE GREAT 'I AM' OF THE OLD SCRIPTURES, I WORSHIP YOU, HALLELUJAH.
212. THERE IS NOTHING MAN CAN DO TO SEPARATE US LORD, I PRAISE YOU JESUS, HALLELUJAH.
213. SHOW ME THE WAY LORD, I PRAISE YOU JESUS, HALLELUJAH.
214. HELP ME LORD, I PRAISE YOU JESUS, HALLELUJAH.
215. ALL THINGS ARE POSSIBLE LORD, I PRAISE YOU JESUS, HALLELUJAH.
216. LORD YOU ARE ABLE TO DO ALL THINGS, I PRAISE YOU JESUS, HALLELUJAH.
217. I FALL DOWN LORD BUT I GET UP IN YOUR POWER, I PRAISE YOU JESUS, HALLELUJAH.
218. GREAT IS YOUR MERCY LORD, I WORSHIP YOU, JESUS, HALLELUJAH.
219. I BELIEVE IN THE BODY OF THE LORD, I PRAISE YOU JESUS, HALLELUJAH.
220. I BELIEVE IN THE WORSHIP OF THE LORD, I PRAISE YOU JESUS, HALLELUJAH.

221. I BELIEVE IN THE BLOOD OF THE LORD, I PRAISE YOU JESUS, HALLELUJAH.
222. I BELIEVE IN THE LIFE OF THE LORD, I PRAISE YOU JESUS, HALLELUJAH.
223. I BELIEVE IN THE SPIRIT OF THE LORD, I PRAISE YOU JESUS, HALLELUJAH.
224. I BELIEVE IN THE HEART OF THE LORD, I PRAISE YOU JESUS, HALLELUJAH.
225. I BELIEVE IN THE FATHER OF THE LORD, I PRAISE YOU JESUS, HALLELUJAH.
226. I BELIEVE IN THE WILL OF THE LORD, I PRAISE YOU JESUS, HALLELUJAH.
227. I BELIEVE IN THE AUTHORITY OF THE LORD, I PRAISE YOU JESUS, HALLELUJAH.
228. I BELIEVE IN THE LOVE OF THE LORD, I PRAISE YOU JESUS, HALLELUJAH.
229. I BELIEVE IN THE GRACE OF THE LORD, I PRAISE YOU JESUS, HALLELUJAH.
230. I BELIEVE IN THE JOY OF THE LORD, I PRAISE YOU JESUS, HALLELUJAH.
231. I BELIEVE IN THE INSPIRATION OF THE LORD, I PRAISE YOU JESUS, HALLELUJAH.
232. I BELIEVE IN THE LIGHT OF THE LORD, I PRAISE YOU JESUS, HALLELUJAH.
233. I BELIEVE IN THE FAITH OF THE LORD, I PRAISE YOU JESUS, HALLELUJAH.
234. I BELIEVE IN THE UNDERSTANDING OF THE LORD, I PRAISE YOU JESUS, HALLELUJAH.
235. I BELIEVE IN THE PRAISES OF THE LORD, I PRAISE YOU JESUS, HALLELUJAH.
236. I BELIEVE IN THE SONG OF THE LORD, I PRAISE YOU JESUS, HALLELUJAH.
237. I BELIEVE IN THE SON OF THE LIVING GOD, I PRAISE YOU JESUS, HALLELUJAH.
238. I BELIEVE IN THE BLESSINGS OF THE LORD, I PRAISE YOU JESUS, HALLELUJAH.

239. YOUR GREATEST ACT LORD WAS TO DECIEVE THE GREAT DECIEVER, I PRAISE YOU JESUS, HALLELUJAH.
240. HAVE MERCY ON ME JESUS FOR I SIN AGAINST YOU ALONE, I PRAISE YOU ALONE, HALLELUJAH.
241. HAVE MERCY ON ME JESUS FOR I SIN AGAINST YOU ALONE, I PRAISE YOU ALONE, HALLELUJAH.
242. HAVE MERCY ON ME JESUS FOR I SIN AGAINST YOU ALONE, I PRAISE YOU ALONE, HALLELUJAH.
243. LORD GOD ALMIGHTY JESUS CHRIST, I PRAISE YOU, HALLELUJAH.
244. LORD GOD ALMIGHTY JESUS CHRIST, I PRAISE YOU, HALLELUJAH.
245. LORD GOD ALMIGHTY JESUS CHRIST, I PRAISE YOU, HALLELUJAH.
246. I PRAISE YOU JESUS, HALLELUJAH.
247. I NEED YOU JESUS TO SURVIVE LORD, HALLELUJAH.
248. I LOVE YOU JESUS, HALLELUJAH.
249. YOU ARE IMPORTANT TO ME JESUS, HALLELUJAH.
250. COME TO ME JESUS, HALLELUJAH.
251. LET ME FEEL YOU JESUS, HALLELUJAH.
252. I AM HAPPY TO BE PART OF YOUR BODY JESUS, I PRAISE YOU, HALLELUJAH.
253. STAND WITH ME JESUS, HALLELUJAH.
254. YOU ARE GREAT JESUS, HALLELUJAH.
255. YOU ARE HOLY JESUS, HALLELUJAH.
256. YOU ARE FAITHFUL JESUS, HALLELUJAH.
257. JESUS YOU ARE MY LORD AND MY GOD, HALLELUJAH.
258. JESUS YOU ARE THE KING OF HEAVEN AND EARTH, I PRAISE YOU, HALLELUJAH.
259. YOU ARE WONDERFUL JESUS, HALLELUJAH.
260. YOU ARE MARVELOUS JESUS, HALLELUJAH.

261. I CALL YOU RIGHTEOUS JESUS, HALLELUJAH.
262. I CALL YOU AWESOME JESUS, HALLELUJAH.
263. YOU ARE WORHTY OF ALL PRAISE JESUS, HALLELUJAH.
264. YOU ARE MERCIFUL JESUS, HALLELUJAH.
265. JESUS YOU ARE THE ALPHA AND OMEGA, I PRAISE YOU, HALLELUJAH.
266. YOU ARE THE PEACE MAKER JESUS, HALLELUJAH.
267. YOU ARE THE GLORIOUS JESUS, HALLELUJAH.
268. YOU ARE THE HEALER JESUS, HALLELUJAH.
269. YOU ARE THE LOVING JESUS, HALLELUJAH.
270. YOU ARE THE ROCK JESUS, HALLELUJAH.
271. COME AND HOLD ME JESUS, HALLELUJAH.
272. COME AND LOVE ME JESUS, HALLELUJAH.
273. I CAN'T DO WITHOUT YOU JESUS, HALLELUJAH.
274. SHOW YOURSELF TO ME JESUS, HALLELUJAH.
275. I WORSHIP YOU JESUS, HALLELUJAH.
276. I HONOR YOU JESUS, HALLELUJAH.
277. GREAT IS YOUR MERCY TOWARDS ME JESUS, HALLELUJAH.
278. YOU ARE THE GREAT PROVIDER JESUS, HALLELUJAH.
279. I THANK YOU FOR YOUR KINDNESS JESUS, HALLELUJAH.
280. THANKS FOR BEING MY SAVIOR JESUS, HALLELUJAH.
281. I PRAISE YOUR SPIRIT JESUS, HALLELUJAH.
282. I THANK YOU JESUS FOR GIVING ME ETERNAL LIFE, HALLELUJAH.
283. THANKS FOR BEING JUST TO ME JESUS, HALLELUJAH.
284. I THANK YOU JESUS FOR UNDERSTANDING MY NEEDS, I PRAISE YOU, HALLELUJAH.
285. I PRAISE YOU LORD GOD ALMIGHTY JESUS CHRIST, HALLELUJAH.

286. I PRAISE YOU LORD GOD ALMIGHTY JESUS CHRIST, HALLELUJAH.
287. I PRAISE YOU LORD GOD ALMIGHTY JESUS CHRIST, HALLELUJAH.
288. JESUS YOU ARE WORTHY OF ALL THE GLORY AND ALL THE PRAISE, HALLELUJAH.
289. THERE IS NONE LIKE YOU LORD JESUS, HALLELUJAH.
290. YOU ARE HOLY LORD GOD ALMIGHTY JESUS CHRIST, HALLELUJAH.
291. YOU ARE HOLY LORD GOD ALMIGHTY JESUS CHRIST, HALLELUJAH.
292. YOU ARE HOLY LORD GOD ALMIGHTY JESUS CHRIST, HALLELUJAH.
293. YOU ARE THE LAMB ON THE THRONE JESUS, HALLELUJAH.
294. JESUS YOU ARE THE ONE AND ONLY SON OF GOD THE MOST HIGH, HALLELUJAH.
295. I WANT YOU TO TOUCH ME JESUS, HALLELUJAH.
296. I WANT YOU TO NEVER LEAVE ME JESUS, HALLELUJAH.
297. I WANT YOU TO ALWAYS BE IN MY LIFE LORD JESUS, HALLELUJAH.
298. I NEED YOU NOW LORD JESUS, I PRAISE YOU, HALLELUJAH.
299. JESUS YOU ARE THE KING OF KINGS, HALLELUJAH.
300. JESUS YOU ARE THE LORD OF LORDS, HALLELUJAH.
301. JESUS I KNOW YOU LIVE TODAY, I PRAISE YOU, HALLELUJAH.
302. JESUS I KNOW YOU WILL LIVE TOMORROW, I PRAISE YOU, HALLELUJAH.
303. JESUS THE GOD OF THE BIBLE IS GREAT AND GENEROUS, HALLELUJAH.
304. COME TO ME LORD JESUS LET ME SEE YOU, HALLELUJAH.

305. I WANT YOU TO HOLD ME LORD JESUS, HALLELUJAH.
306. I WANT TO FEEL YOUR LOVE LORD JESUS, HALLELUJAH.
307. JESUS YOU ARE THE CENTER OF MY JOY, I PRAISE YOU, HALLELUJAH.
308. HOLY HOLY HOLY IS THE LORD ALMIGHTY JESUS CHRIST, HALLELUJAH.
309. HOLY HOLY HOLY IS THE LORD ALMIGHTY JESUS CHRIST, HALLELUJAH.
310. HOLY HOLY HOLY IS THE LORD ALMIGHTY JESUS CHRIST, HALLELUJAH.
311. JESUS YOU ARE THE MAJOR PRESENCE IN MY LIFE, HALLELUJAH.
312. JESUS I NEED YOU NOW, HALLELUJAH.
313. JESUS COME RESCUE ME, HALLELUJAH.
314. JESUS DON'T WAIT ONE SECOND BEFORE YOU COME, HALLELUJAH.
315. JESUS I WANT TO SERVE YOU ALONE, HALLELUJAH.
316. LORD GOD ALMIGHTY JESUS CHRIST, I PRAISE YOU, HALLELUJAH.
317. LORD GOD ALMIGHTY JESUS CHRIST, I PRAISE YOU, HALLELUJAH.
318. LORD GOD ALMIGHTY JESUS CHRIST, I PRAISE YOU, HALLELUJAH.
319. I HONOR YOU JESUS, I PRAISE YOU, HALLELUJAH.
320. I WILL CONFORM TO YOUR BLESSED WAYS LORD JESUS, HALLELUJAH.
321. GREAT IS YOUR WILL AND YOUR MERCY MY LORD JESUS, I PRAISE YOU, HALLELUJAH.
322. JESUS YOU ARE EVER FAITHFUL, I PRAISE YOU, HALLELUJAH.
323. DEAR JESUS YOU ARE THE GREAT "I AM," I PRAISE YOU, HALLELUJAH.
324. JESUS YOUR TENDER MERCY GIVE ME PEACE, I PRAISE YOU, HALLELUJAH.

325. JESUS YOU ARE THE MIRACLE WORKER, I PRAISE YOU, HALLELUJAH.
326. JESUS YOU ARE THE HEALER, I PRAISE YOU, HALLELUJAH.
327. HOSANNA IN THE HIGHEST! I PRAISE YOU JESUS, HALLELUJAH.
328. HOSANNA IN THE HIGHEST! BLESSED IS HE WHO COMES IN THE NAME OF THE LORD! I PRAISE YOU JESUS, HALLELUJAH.
329. HOSANNA TO THE SON OF DAVID, I PRAISE YOU JESUS, HALLELUJAH.
330. JESUS YOU DIED, TO SAVE ME, I PRAISE YOU, HALLELUJAH.
331. JESUS YOU DIED, SO I AM HEALED, I PRAISE YOU, HALLELUJAH.
332. JESUS YOU DIED, SO I OBTAIN GLORY, I PRAISE YOU, HALLELUJAH.
333. JESUS YOU DIED, SO I OBTAIN LIFE, I PRAISE YOU, HALLELUJAH.
334. JESUS YOU DIED, TO MAKE ME HAPPY, I PRAISE YOU, HALLELUJAH.
335. JESUS YOU DIED, TO GIVE ME HOPE, I PRAISE YOU, HALLELUJAH.
336. JESUS YOU DIED, TO GIVE ME YOUR RIGHTEOUSNESS, I PRAISE YOU, HALLELUJAH.
337. JESUS YOU DIED, FOR US TO BE TOGETHER, I PRAISE YOU, HALLELUJAH.
338. JESUS YOU DIED, TO FREE ME FROM SIN, I PRAISE YOU, HALLELUJAH.
339. JESUS YOU DIED, TO GIVE ME ETERNAL LIFE, I PRAISE YOU, HALLELUJAH.
340. JESUS YOU DIED, TO PROSPER ME, I PRAISE YOU, HALLELUJAH.
341. JESUS YOU DIED, FOR ME TO DEVELOP A RELATIONSHIP WITH YOU, I PRAISE YOU, HALLELUJAH.

342. JESUS YOU DIED, FOR ME TO DEVELOP A RELATIONSHIP WITH OUR FATHER GOD, I PRAISE YOU, HALLELUJAH.
343. JESUS YOU DIED, FOR ME TO HAVE A RELATIONSHIP WITH THE HOLY SPIRIT, I PRAISE YOU, HALLELUJAH.
344. JESUS YOU DIED, TO SHOW ME ALL THE SECRETS OF HEAVEN, I PRAISE YOU, HALLELUJAH.
345. JESUS YOU DIED, FOR ME TO KNOW WHAT TRUE LOVE IS, I PRAISE YOU, HALLELUJAH.
346. JESUS YOU DIED, SO I KNOW WHAT TRUE OBEDIENCE IS, I PRAISE YOU, HALLELUJAH.
347. JESUS I KNOW YOU LIVE TODAY, I PRAISE YOU, HALLELUJAH.
348. THERE IS NO GOD LIKE YOU JESUS, I PRAISE YOU, HALLELUJAH.
349. PURIFY ME JESUS, I PRAISE YOU, HALLELUJAH.
350. MAKE YOURSELF KNOWN TO ME JESUS, I PRAISE YOU, HALLELUJAH.
351. JESUS YOUR HEART IS CLEAN AND JUST, I PRAISE YOU, HALLELUJAH.
352. WHEN I CALL YOUR NAME JESUS YOU NEVER SAY NO, I PRAISE YOU, HALLELUJAH.
353. YOU HAVE PROMISED TO BLESS ME IF I OBEY YOU, I PRAISE YOU LORD JESUS, HALLELUJAH.
354. YOU HAVE PROMISED TO COME NEAR ME IF I COME NEAR YOU, I PRAISE YOU LORD JESUS, HALLELUJAH.
355. YOU HAVE PROMISED TO WATCH OVER AND COUNSEL ME, I PRAISE YOU LORD JESUS, HALLELUJAH.
356. YOU PROMISED NOT A HAIR ON MY HEAD WILL PERISH, I PRAISE YOU LORD JESUS, HALLELUJAH.
357. YOU PROMISED, IF I CALL ON YOU IN TIMES OF TROUBLE; YOU WILL DELIVER ME AND HONOR ME, I PRAISE YOU JESUS, HALLELUJAH.

358. YOU PROMISED TO NEVER FORSAKE ME OR LEAVE ME, I PRAISE YOU LORD JESUS, HALLELUJAH.
359. YOU PROMISED THAT IF I CONFESS MY SINS, YOU WILL BE FAITHFUL AND JUST TO ME, AND YOU WILL FORGIVE ME OF MY SINS AND PURIFY ME FROM ALL UNRIGHTEOUSNESS, I PRAISE YOU LORD JESUS, HALLELUJAH.
360. ONLY YOU ARE HOLY JESUS, I PRAISE YOU LORD, HALLELUJAH.
361. ONLY YOU ARE HOLY JESUS, I PRAISE YOU LORD, HALLELUJAH.
362. ONLY YOU ARE HOLY JESUS, I PRAISE YOU LORD, HALLELUJAH.
363. THE SPIRIT OF GOD IS ON YOU JESUS, I PRAISE YOU LORD, HALLELUJAH.
364. GOD THE FATHER HAS ANOINTED YOU JESUS, I PRAISE YOU LORD, HALLELUJAH.
365. JESUS YOU PREACHED GOOD NEWS TO THE POOR, I PRAISE YOU LORD, HALLELUJAH.
366. JESUS YOU CAME TO PROCLAIM FREEDOM FOR THE PRISONERS, I PRAISE YOU LORD, HALLELUJAH.
367. RECOVERY OF SIGHT FOR THE BLIND, YOU PROVIDED JESUS, I PRAISE YOU LORD, HALLELUJAH.
368. YOU RAISED THE DEAD LORD JESUS, I WORSHIP YOU, HALLELUJAH.
369. JESUS, YOU RELEASED THE OPPRESSED, I PRAISE YOU LORD, HALLELUJAH.
370. JESUS YOU PROCLAIM THE YEAR OF THE LORD'S FAVOR, I PRAISE YOU LORD, HALLELUJAH.
371. YOUR GREATEST PLEASURE JESUS IS FOR US TO BELIEVE YOU, I BELIEVE YOU AND PRAISE YOU LORD JESUS, HALLELUJAH.
372. I DO NOT DOUBT YOU JESUS, I PRAISE YOU LORD, HALLELUJAH.

373. MY LORD JESUS YOU ARE THE GREAT LION OF JUDAH, HALLELUJAH.
374. OH JESUS HOW POWERFUL YOU ARE, I PRAISE YOU, HALLELUJAH.
375. YOU ARE HOLY, LORD JESUS, I PRAISE YOUR HOLY NAME, HALLELUJAH.
376. YOU ARE HOLY, LORD JESUS, I PRAISE YOUR HOLY NAME, HALLELUJAH.
377. YOU ARE HOLY, MY GOD JESUS, I PRAISE YOUR HOLY NAME, HALLELUJAH.
378. JESUS YOU ARE THE SUN OF MAN, I PRAISE YOUR HOLY NAME, HALLELUJAH.
379. MY LOVING JESUS BE WITH ME LORD JESUS, I PRAISE YOUR HOLY NAME, HALLELUJAH.
380. STAY WITH ME LORD JESUS, HALLELUJAH.
381. NEVER LEAVE ME LORD JESUS, HALLELUJAH.
382. I HAVE TO HAVE YOU WITH ME LORD JESUS, HALLELUJAH.
383. I WANT YOU WITH ME LORD JESUS, I PRAISE YOUR HOLY NAME, HALLELUJAH.
384. I LOVE YOU LORD JESUS, I PRAISE YOUR HOLY NAME, HALLELUJAH.
385. I WANT YOUR INTENSE LOVE, LORD JESUS, HALLELUJAH.
386. SHOW YOURSELF TO ME LOVING JESUS, HALLELUJAH.
387. YOU MADE THE HEAVENS AND THE EARTH, I PRAISE YOUR HOLY NAME JESUS, HALLELUJAH.
388. MY KING IS MY GREATEST POSSESSION, I PRAISE YOU JESUS, HALLELUJAH.
389. MY REDEEMER FROM EVERLASTING IS YOUR NAME, JESUS, HALLELUJAH.
390. YOU ARE AWESOME, YOU ARE AWESOME MY GOD AND LORD JESUS, HALLELUJAH .
391. I LOVE YOU JESUS, HALLELUJAH.
392. I LIFT MY HANDS UP TO YOU JESUS, I PRAISE YOU, HALLELUJAH.

393. MELODIES FROM HEAVEN RAIN DOWN ON ME, I PRAISE YOUR HOLY NAME JESUS, HALLELUJAH.
394. GIVE ME ALL YOUR JOY LORD, I PRAISE YOU JESUS, HALLELUJAH.
395. THANKS FOR YOUR PEACE, I PRAISE YOU JESUS, HALLELUJAH.
396. I THANK YOU FOR THE HOLY SPIRIT, I PRAISE YOU JESUS, HALLELUJAH.
397. I THANK YOU FOR YOUR BLESSINGS LORD, I PRAISE YOU JESUS, HALLELUJAH.
398. I THANK FOR GIVING ME UNDERSTANDING, I PRAISE YOU JESUS, HALLELUJAH.
399. I THANK YOU FOR WISDOM, I PRAISE YOU JESUS, HALLELUJAH.
400. I THANK YOU FOR LONG LIFE, I PRAISE YOU JESUS, HALLELUJAH.
401. I THANK YOU FOR GREAT HEALTH, I PRAISE YOU JESUS, HALLELUJAH.
402. I THANK YOU FOR CHOSING ME FOR SALVATION, I PRAISE YOU JESUS, HALLELUJAH.
403. YOUR LOVE IS EVERLASTING, I PRAISE YOU JESUS, HALLELUJAH.
404. NO ONE CAN LOVE ME LIKE YOU LORD, I PRAISE YOU JESUS, HALLELUJAH.
405. NO ONE KNOWS ME LIKE YOU, I PRAISE YOU JESUS, HALLELUJAH.
406. YOU ARE ALWAYS IN MY LIFE LORD, I PRAISE YOU JESUS, HALLELUJAH.
407. YOU ARE ALWAYS GIVING ME A LIFE LINE LORD, I PRAISE YOU JESUS, HALLELUJAH.
408. I WILL PRAISE YOU JESUS FOREVER, HALLELUJAH.
409. THE SWORD OF THE SPIRIT COMES FROM YOU JESUS, I PRAISE YOU, HALLELUJAH.
410. JESUS YOU ARE THE GREAT 'I AM' OF THE OLD SCRIPTURES, I PRAISE YOU, HALLELUJAH .

411. THERE IS NOTHING MAN CAN DO TO SEPARATE US, I PRAISE YOU JESUS, HALLELUJAH.
412. SHOW ME THE WAY LORD, I PRAISE YOU JESUS, HALLELUJAH.
413. HELP ME LORD, I PRAISE YOU JESUS, HALLELUJAH.
414. ALL THINGS ARE POSSIBLE LORD, I PRAISE YOU JESUS, HALLELUJAH.
415. LORD YOU ARE ABLE, I PRAISE YOU JESUS, HALLELUJAH.
416. WE FALL DOWN LORD BUT WE GET UP WITH YOUR POWER LORD, I PRAISE YOU JESUS, HALLELUJAH.
417. I BELIEVE IN THE BODY OF THE LORD, I PRAISE YOU JESUS, HALLELUJAH.
418. I BELIEVE IN THE WORSHIP OF THE LORD, I PRAISE YOU JESUS, HALLELUJAH.
419. I BELIEVE IN THE BLOOD OF THE LORD, I PRAISE YOU JESUS, HALLELUJAH.
420. I BELIEVE IN THE LIFE OF THE LORD, I PRAISE YOU JESUS, HALLELUJAH.
421. I BELIEVE IN THE SPIRIT OF THE LORD, I PRAISE YOU JESUS, HALLELUJAH.
422. I BELIEVE IN THE HEART OF THE LORD, I PRAISE YOU JESUS,HALLELUJAH.
423. I BELIEVE IN THE FATHER OF THE LORD, I PRAISE YOU JESUS, HALLELUJAH.
424. I BELIEVE IN THE WILL OF THE LORD, I PRAISE YOU JESUS, HALLELUJAH.
425. I BELIEVE IN THE AUTHORITY OF THE LORD, I PRAISE YOU JESUS, HALLELUJAH.
426. I BELIEVE IN THE LOVE OF THE LORD, I PRAISE YOU JESUS, HALLELUJAH.
427. I BELIEVE IN THE GRACE OF THE LORD, I PRAISE YOU JESUS, HALLELUJAH.
428. I BELIEVE IN THE JOY OF THE LORD, I PRAISE YOU JESUS, HALLELUJAH.

429. I BELIEVE IN THE INSPIRATION OF THE LORD, I PRAISE YOU JESUS, HALLELUJAH.

430. I BELIEVE IN THE LIGHT OF THE LORD, I PRAISE YOU JESUS, HALLELUJAH.

431. I BELIEVE IN THE FAITH OF THE LORD, I PRAISE YOU JESUS, HALLELUJAH.

432. I BELIEVE IN THE UNDERSTANDING OF THE LORD, I PRAISE YOU JESUS, HALLELUJAH.

433. I BELIEVE IN THE PRAISES OF THE LORD, I PRAISE YOU JESUS, HALLELUJAH.

434. I BELIEVE IN THE SONG OF THE LORD, I PRAISE YOU JESUS, HALLELUJAH.

435. I BELIEVE IN THE SON OF THE LIVING GOD, I PRAISE YOU JESUS, HALLELUJAH.

436. I BELIEVE IN THE BLESSINGS OF THE LORD, I PRAISE YOU JESUS, HALLELUJAH.

437. I BELIEVE IN THE OBEDIENCE OF THE LORD, I PRAISE YOU JESUS, HALLELUJAH.

438. HOSANNA IN THE HIGHEST! I PRAISE YOU JESUS, HALLELUJAH.

439. HOSANNA IN THE HIGHEST! BLESSED IS HE WHO COMES IN THE NAME OF THE LORD! I PRAISE YOU JESUS, HALLELUJAH.

440. HOSANNA TO THE SON OF DAVID, I PRAISE YOU JESUS, HALLELUJAH.

441. I THANK YOU FOR YOUR GUIDANCE, I WORSHIP YOU JESUS, HALLELUJAH.

442. I THANK YOU FOR PROTECTION, I WORSHIP YOU JESUS, HALLELUJAH.

443. I THANK YOU FOR YOUR KINGDOM, I WORSHIP YOU JESUS, HALLELUJAH.

444. I THANK YOU FOR OUR RELATIONSHIP, I WORSHIP YOU JESUS, HALLELUJAH.

445. I THANK YOU FOR MY HAPPINESS, I WORSHIP YOU JESUS, HALLELUJAH.

446. I THANK YOU FOR YOUR GLORY, I WORSHIP YOU JESUS, HALLELUJAH.

447. I THANK YOU FOR MY PRIESTHOOD, I WORSHIP YOU JESUS, HALLELUJAH.
448. I THANK YOU FOR MY ANOINTING, I WORSHIP YOU JESUS, HALLELUJAH.
449. I THANK YOU FOR YOUR MERCY, I WORSHIP YOU JESUS, HALLELUJAH.
450. I THANK YOU FOR MY SALVATION, I WORSHIP YOU JESUS, HALLELUJAH.
451. I THANK YOU FOR MY KNOWLEDGE, I WORSHIP YOU JESUS, HALLELUJAH.
452. I THANK YOU FOR MY UNDERSTANDING, I WORSHIP YOU JESUS, HALLELUJAH.
453. I THANK YOU FOR REMOVING ALL CURSES FROM MY LIFE, I WORSHIP YOU JESUS, HALLELUJAH.
454. I THANK YOU FOR ASSIGNING ANGELS TO ME, I WORSHIP YOU JESUS, HALLELUJAH.
455. I THANK YOU FOR GIVING ME A SPIRITUAL TONGUE, I WORSHIP YOU JESUS, HALLELUJAH.
456. I THANK YOU FOR ALL YOUR GIFTS, I WORSHIP YOU JESUS, HALLELUJAH.
457. I THANK YOU FOR YOUR HOLINESS, I WORSHIP YOU JESUS, HALLELUJAH.
458. I THANK YOU FOR THE MUSIC OF THE WORLD, I WORSHIP YOU JESUS, HALLELUJAH.
459. I THANK YOU FOR THE PEACE IN THE WORLD, I WORSHIP YOU JESUS, HALLELUJAH.
460. I THANK YOU FOR THE PROTECTION OF ISRAEL, I WORSHIP YOU JESUS, HALLELUJAH.
461. I THANK YOU FOR THE PROTECTION OF THE POOR, I WORSHIP YOU JESUS, HALLELUJAH.
462. I THANK YOU FOR LIFE, I WORSHIP YOU JESUS, HALLELUJAH.
463. I THANK YOU FOR ETERNAL LIFE, I WORSHIP YOU JESUS, HALLELUJAH.
464. I THANK YOU FOR THE HOLY SPIRIT, I WORSHIP YOU JESUS, HALLELUJAH.

465. I THANK YOU FOR ACCEPTING MY UNDEFILED OFFERINGS, I WORSHIP YOU JESUS, HALLELUJAH.

466. I THANK YOU FOR SHEDDING YOUR BLOOD FOR ME, I WORSHIP YOU JESUS, HALLELUJAH.

467. I THANK YOU FOR YOUR EXALTATION, I WORSHIP YOU JESUS, HALLELUJAH.

468. I THANK YOU FOR GIVING ME ACCESS TO HEAVEN, I WORSHIP YOU JESUS, HALLELUJAH.

469. I THANK YOU FOR OVERCOMING ALL DISEASES, I WORSHIP YOU JESUS, HALLELUJAH.

470. I THANK YOU FOR YOUR MIRACLES, I WORSHIP YOU JESUS, HALLELUJAH.

471. I THANK YOU FOR PROTECTING THE WIDOW, I WORSHIP YOU JESUS, HALLELUJAH.

472. I THANK YOU FOR PROTECTING THE CHILDREN, I WORSHIP YOU JESUS, HALLELUJAH.

473. I KNOW YOU LIVE TODAY LORD, I WORSHIP YOU JESUS, HALLELUJAH.

474. I KNOW YOU ARE WAITING FOR ME TO SEEK YOU LORD, I WORSHIP YOU JESUS, HALLELUJAH.

475. I KNOW YOU WANT TO SHOW YOURSELF TO ME LORD, I WORSHIP YOU JESUS, HALLELUJAH.

476. YOU ARE THE ALPHA AND OMEGA LORD, I WORSHIP YOU JESUS, HALLELUJAH.

477. NOTHING WAS MADE WITHOUT YOUR KNOWLEDGE LORD, I WORSHIP YOU JESUS, HALLELUJAH.

478. YOU AND THE FATHER JEHOVAH ARE ONE LORD, I WORSHIP YOU JESUS, HALLELUJAH.

479. YOU ARE THE KING OF KINGS AND THE LORD OF LORDS, I WORSHIP YOU JESUS, HALLELUJAH.

480. YOU ARE HE WHO SITS ON THE THRONE, I WORSHIP YOU JESUS, HALLELUJAH.

481. YOU ARE THE HOLY ONE OF ISRAEL, I WORSHIP YOU JESUS, HALLELUJAH.

482. YOU ARE THE ONE THAT THE MAGI WORSHIPED, I PRAISE YOU JESUS, HALLELUJAH.

483. YOU ARE THE BRIGHT MORNING STAR, I PRAISE YOU JESUS, HALLELUJAH.

484. YOU ARE THE TRUE KING OF THE JEWS, I PRAISE YOU JESUS, HALLELUJAH.

485. YOU ARE THE MESSIAH TO COME, I PRAISE YOU JESUS, HALLELUJAH.

486. YOU ARE THE ONLY SON OF GOD, I PRAISE YOU JESUS, HALLELUJAH.

487. YOU WERE BORN FROM THE VIRGIN MARY, I WORSHIP YOU JESUS, HALLELUJAH.

488. YOUR NAME IS EMANUEL, GOD WITH ME, I PRAISE YOU JESUS, HALLELUJAH.

489. I PRAISE YOU JESUS, WHO WAS BORN IN BETHLEHEM, HALLELUJAH.

490. I PRAISE YOU JESUS, WHO WAS BAPTIZED BY JOHN THE BAPTIST, HALLELUJAH.

491. I PRAISE YOU JESUS, WHO HAS THE FULL RIGHTEOUSNESS OF GOD, HALLELUJAH.

492. I PRAISE YOU JESUS, WHO OVERCAME ALL TEMPTATIONS, HALLELUJAH.

493. YOU ARE THE ONE WHO PREACHED REPENT FOR THE KINGDOM OF GOD IS NEAR, I PRAISE YOU JESUS, HALLELUJAH.

494. YOU CHOSE THE TWELVE DISCIPLES, I PRAISE YOU JESUS HALLELUJAH.

495. YES LORD, YOU THOUGHT YOUR DISCIPLES HOW TO BE FISHERS OF MEN, I PRAISE YOU JESUS HALLELUJAH.

496. JESUS YOU HEALED ALL THE DISEASED AND SICK PEOPLE YOU FOUND, I PRAISE YOU JESUS.

497. LORD YOU HELPED ALL THOSE WITH FAITH IN YOU, I PRAISE YOU JESUS.

498. YOU HEALED EVERYONE THAT BELIEVED, I BELIEVE, I PRAISE YOU JESUS.

499. I WILL WORK HARD FOR YOU LORD, I PRAISE YOU JESUS.
500. LORD YOU CALM THE STORMS AND THE WINDS, I PRAISE YOU JESUS.
501. LORD YOU DROVE OUT DEMONS, I PRAISE YOU JESUS.
502. LORD YOU MADE THE BLIND SEE AND MUTE TALK, I PRAISE YOU JESUS.
503. LORD YOU GAVE YOUR TWELVE DISCIPLES AUTHORITY TO DRIVE OUT EVIL SPIRITS AND TO HEAL EVERY DISEASE AND SICKNESS, I PRAISE YOU JESUS.
504. LORD YOU SAID YOU WILL DELIVER ME AND THAT IS WHAT I BELIEVE, I PRAISE YOU JESUS.
505. LORD YOU DID IT JUST FOR ME, I PRAISE YOU JESUS.
506. JOHN THE BAPTIST TALKED ABOUT YOU LORD, I PRAISE YOU JESUS.
507. ABRAHAM SAW YOU LORD AND HE WAS GLAD, I PRAISE YOU JESUS.
508. WOE TO THOSE WHO DON'T REPENT BUT, I WILL LORD, I PRAISE YOU JESUS.
509. I PRAISE YOU JESUS, FOR REVEALING THE WISE THINGS TO ME, HALLELUJAH.
510. LORD I HONOR YOU AND I PRAISE YOU JESUS, HALLELUJAH.
511. LORD TEACH ME TO WALK ON WATER, I PRAISE YOU JESUS.
512. I PRAISE YOU JESUS FOR SHOWING ME HOW GREAT MIRACLES COULD BE DONE.
513. I PRAISE YOU JESUS FOR BEING THE GOD OF ALL GODS.
514. I PRAISE YOU JESUS FOR SUPPLYING MY EVERY NEED.
515. I PRAISE YOU JESUS FOR BEING MY ADVOCATE.
516. I PRAISE YOU JESUS FOR PRAYING FOR MY SALVATION.

517. LORD YOU CARRY A NAME ABOVE ALL OTHER NAMES, I PRAISE YOU JESUS.
518. HOSANNA IN THE HIGHEST! I PRAISE YOU JESUS, HALLELUJAH.
519. HOSANNA IN THE HIGHEST! BLESSED IS HE WHO COMES IN THE NAME OF THE LORD! I PRAISE YOU JESUS, HALLELUJAH.
520. HOSANNA TO THE SON OF DAVID. I PRAISE YOU JESUS, HALLELUJAH.
521. HOLY HOLY HOLY IS THE LORD GOD ALMIGHTY JESUS CHRIST, I PRAISE YOU JESUS.
522. HOLY HOLY HOLY IS THE LORD GOD ALMIGHTY JESUS CHRIST, I PRAISE YOU JESUS.
523. HOLY HOLY HOLY IS THE LORD GOD ALMIGHTY JESUS CHRIST, I PRAISE YOU JESUS.
524. HOLY HOLY HOLY IS THE LORD GOD ALMIGHTY JESUS CHRIST, I PRAISE YOU JESUS.
525. HOLY HOLY HOLY IS THE LORD GOD ALMIGHTY JESUS CHRIST, I PRAISE YOU JESUS.
526. HOLY HOLY HOLY IS THE LORD GOD ALMIGHTY JESUS CHRIST, I PRAISE YOU JESUS.
527. HOLY HOLY HOLY IS THE LORD GOD ALMIGHTY JESUS CHRIST, I PRAISE YOU JESUS.
528. HALLELUJAH, HALLELUJAH, HALLELUJAH, I PRAISE YOU JESUS.
529. HALLELUJAH, HALLELUJAH, HALLELUJAH, I PRAISE YOU JESUS.
530. HALLELUJAH, HALLELUJAH, HALLELUJAH, I PRAISE YOU JESUS.
531. HALLELUJAH, HALLELUJAH, HALLELUJAH, I PRAISE YOU JESUS.
532. HALLELUJAH, HALLELUJAH, HALLELUJAH, I PRAISE YOU JESUS.
533. HALLELUJAH, HALLELUJAH, HALLELUJAH, I PRAISE YOU JESUS.
534. HALLELUJAH, HALLELUJAH, HALLELUJAH, I PRAISE YOU JESUS.

535. GREAT IS YOUR MERCY LORD, I PRAISE YOU JESUS.
536. LORD YOU ARE THE ORIGINAL SON OF MAN, I PRAISE YOU JESUS, HALLELUJAH.
537. I LOVE YOU JESUS, I PRAISE YOU GOD, HALLELUJAH.
538. ONLY YOU ARE HOLY, I PRAISE YOU JESUS.
539. ONLY YOU ARE HOLY, I PRAISE YOU JESUS, HALLELUJAH.
540. ONLY YOU ARE HOLY, I PRAISE YOU JEHOVAH GOD, HALLELUJAH
541. ONLY YOU ARE HOLY JESUS, HALLELUJAH.
542. JESUS YOU WERE PRESENT, WHEN THERE WERE NO DEPTHS, HALLELUJAH.
543. JESUS YOU WERE PRESENT, WHEN THERE WERE NO SPRINGS ABOUNDING WITH WATER, HALLELUJAH.
544. JESUS YOU WERE PRESENT, BEFORE THE MOUNTAINS WERE SETTLED, HALLELUJAH.
545. JESUS YOU WERE PRESENT, BEFORE THE HILLS WERE BROUGHT FORTH, HALLELUJAH
546. JESUS YOU WERE PRESENT, WHILE GOD THE FATHER HAD NOT YET MADE THE EARTH AND THE FIELDS, HALLELUJAH.
547. JESUS YOU WERE PRESENT, BEFORE THE FIRST DUST OF THE WORLD, HALLELUJAH.
548. JESUS YOU WERE PRESENT, WHEN GOD THE FATHER ESTABLISHED THE HEAVENS, HALLELUJAH.
549. JESUS YOU WERE PRESENT, WHEN GOD THE FATHER INSCRIBED A CIRCLE ON THE FACE OF THE DEEP, HALLELUJAH.
550. JESUS YOU WERE PRESENT, WHEN GOD THE FATHER MADE FIRM THE SKIES ABOVE, HALLELUJAH.
551. JESUS YOU WERE PRESENT, WHEN THE SPRINGS OF THE DEEP BECAME FIXED, HALLELUJAH.

552. JESUS YOU WERE PRESENT, WHEN GOD THE FATHER SET FORT THE SEA AND ITS BOUNDARY, HALLELUJAH.

553. JESUS YOU WERE PRESENT, WHEN GOD THE FATHER MARKED OUT THE FOUNDATIONS OF THE EARTH, HALLELUJAH.

554. JESUS YOU WERE PRESENT, BESIDE GOD THE FATHER, AS A MASTER WORKMAN AND YOU WERE HIS DAILY DELIGHT, HALLELUJAH.

555. JESUS YOU WERE PRESENT, REJOICING ALWAYS BEFORE GOD THE FATHER, HALLELUJAH.

556. JESUS YOU WERE PRESENT, REJOICING IN THE WORLD, HALLELUJAH.

557. JESUS YOU DELIGHTED IN THE SONS OF MEN, HALLELUJAH.

558. JESUS, YOU SAID, SONS OF MEN LISTEN TO ME, I WILL LISTEN TO YOU LORD, HALLELUJAH.

559. JESUS, YOU SAID, BLESSED ARE THEY WHO KEEP MY WAYS, I WILL, I PRAISE YOU, HALLELUJAH.

560. JESUS YOU WERE PRESENT, WHEN THE PIT AND SHEOL WERE CREATED, HALLELUJAH.

561. GLORY TO JESUS THE KING, I PRAISE YOU LORD, HALLELUJAH.

562. JESUS YOU ARE THE GREAT "I AM," HALLELUJAH.

563. I BELIEVE YOU LOVE ME LORD JESUS, HALLELUJAH.

564. I BELIEVE IN YOUR POWER AND TRUTH LORD JESUS, HALLELUJAH.

565. I BELIEVE YOU CAN DO ALL THINGS LORD JESUS, I PRAISE YOU LORD JESUS.

566. I BELIEVE IN THE GLORY OF GOD, I PRAISE YOU LORD JESUS, HALLELUJAH.

567. I BELIEVE YOU CAN RAISE THE DEAD TODAY JUST LIKE YESTERDAY, I PRAISE YOU GOD JESUS.

568. I BELIEVE YOU CAN MAKE THE BLIND SEE AND THE DEAF HEAR LORD JESUS, HALLELUJAH.

569. I BELIEVE YOU CAN MAKE THE CRIPPLE WALK, I PRAISE YOU LORD JESUS.

570. I BELIEVE YOU CAN MAKE THE MENTALLY ILL HEALTHY, I PRAISE YOU LORD JESUS.

571. I BELIEVE YOU CAN MAKE THE DUMB TALK, I PRAISE YOU LORD JESUS.

572. I BELIEVE YOU ARE PRESENT AT ALL TIMES LORD, I PRAISE YOU LORD JESUS.

573. I BELIEVE IN YOUR HEALING POWER LORD JESUS, I PRAISE YOU JESUS.

574. I PRAISE YOU FOR MAKING ME HEIRS WITH YOU LORD, HALLELUJAH JESUS.

575. I BELONG TO GOD AND I AM GLAD, HALLELUJAH JESUS.

576. JESUS YOU MAKE MY DAYS BRIGHT AND MY NIGHTS COMFORTING, HALLELUJAH.

577. JESUS YOU GIVE MY LIFE MEANING, I PRAISE YOU LORD JESUS.

578. WORTHY IS THE LAMB MY LORD AND GOD JESUS, HALLELUJAH.

579. WORTHY IS THE LAMB, YOU ARE HOLY MY LORD AND GOD JESUS, HALLELUJAH.

580. WORTHY IS THE LAMB, I PRAISE YOU LORD JESUS, HALLELUJAH.

581. THERE IS NO ONE ELSE LIKE YOU, I PRAISE YOU LORD JESUS.

582. MY LIFE IS A TESTAMONY TO YOU LORD JESUS CHRIST, HALLELUJAH.

583. I TRUST YOU LORD JESUS, I PRAISE YOU, HALLELUJAH.

584. YOU WALK IN AUTHORITY LORD JESUS, I PRAISE YOU, HALLELUJAH.

585. I CLAP MY HANDS IN PRAISES TO YOU LORD JESUS, HALLELUJAH.

586. I LOVE YOU JESUS WITH MY WHOLE HEART, I PRAISE YOU LORD JESUS.

587. I LEEP FOR JOY WITH YOU IN MY HEART LORD JESUS, HALLELUJAH.

588. I DANCE LIKE DAVID FOR YOU LORD JESUS, HALLELUJAH.
589. YOU SAID YOU WILL DELIVER ME LORD JESUS AND, I BELIEVE YOU, HALLELUJAH.
590. YOU INSPIRE ME LORD JESUS, I PRAISE YOU LORD JESUS.
591. YOU ARE MY WISDOM LORD JESUS, I PRAISE YOU JESUS.
592. YOU ARE MY CREATIVITY LORD JESUS, I PRAISE YOU JESUS.
593. YOU ARE MY DREAMS LORD JESUS, I PRAISE YOU JESUS.
594. YOU ARE MY DESIRES LORD JESUS, I PRAISE YOU JESUS.
595. YOU ARE MY ASPIRATIONS LORD JESUS, I PRAISE YOU JESUS.
596. YOU ARE MY GOALS LORD JESUS, I PRAISE YOU JESUS.
597. JESUS YOU ARE THE BREAD OF ALL LIFE, HALLELUJAH.
598. JESUS YOU WERE THE ROCK IN HOREB, HALLELUJAH.
599. JESUS YOU WERE THE SPIRITUAL ROCK IN THE DESERT, HALLELUJAH.
600. JESUS YOU WERE THE PERFECT ROCK IN THE DESERT, HALLELUJAH.
601. JESUS YOU ARE THE JUST ROCK, HALLELUJAH.
602. JESUS YOU ARE THE UPRIGHT ROCK, HALLELUJAH.
603. JESUS YOU ARE THE RIGHTEOUS ROCK, HALLELUJAH.
604. JESUS YOU ARE THE ROCK FULL OF HONEY, HALLELUJAH.
605. JESUS YOU ARE THE OIL FROM THE FLINTY ROCK, HALLELUJAH.
606. JESUS YOU ARE THE ROCK WHO GAVE BIRTH TO ALL MANKIND, HALLELUJAH.

607. JESUS YOU ARE THE SACRIFICIAL ROCK, HALLELUJAH.
608. THERE IS NO ROCK HOLIER THAN YOU LORD JESUS, HALLELUJAH.
609. I HAVE NO OTHER GOD BUT YOU JESUS, HALLELUJAH.
610. MY LORD JESUS CHRIST LIVES FOREVER, I PRAISE YOU, HALLELUJAH.
611. MY LORD LIVES NOW, PRAISE BE TO MY ROCK, JESUS.
612. YOU ARE MY ROCK AND MY FORTRESS LORD JESUS, HALLELUJAH.
613. YOU ARE MY GUIDE JESUS, I PRAISE YOU LORD JESUS.
614. IN MY GOD JESUS IS MY SALVATION AND GLORY, HALLELUJAH.
615. JESUS YOU ARE THE ROCK OF MY STRENGTH, HALLELUJAH.
616. MY REFUGE IS IN YOU MY LORD JESUS, HALLELUJAH.
617. YOU ARE MY MOST HIGH GOD AND MY REDEEMER LORD JESUS, HALLELUJAH.
618. YOUR GLORY AND MAJESTY WILL PROTECT ME FOREVER LORD JESUS, HALLELUJAH.
619. THE WISE MEN BUILD THEIR HOUSES ON YOUR ROCK LORD JESUS, HALLELUJAH.
620. THE COST OF MY SINS I WILL NEVER KNOW, I THANK YOU AND WORSHIP YOU LORD JESUS, HALLELUJAH.
621. I GIVE YOU THE HIGHEST PRAISE LORD JESUS, HALLELUJAH.
622. LORD JESUS, YOU HAVE SAVED MY SOUL, HALLELUJAH.
623. POUR OUT YOUR SPIRIT ON ME LORD JESUS, HALLELUJAH.
624. LORD JESUS WHEN I THINK OF YOU I DANCE WITH JOY, HALLELUJAH.

625. JESUS YOU DIED, TO SAVE ME, I PRAISE YOU LORD JESUS, HALLELUJAH.
626. JESUS YOU DIED, SO I AM HEALED, I PRAISE YOU LORD JESUS, HALLELUJAH.
627. JESUS YOU DIED, SO I OBTAIN GLORY, I PRAISE YOU LORD JESUS, HALLELUJAH.
628. JESUS YOU DIED, SO I OBTAIN LIFE, I PRAISE YOU LORD JESUS, HALLELUJAH.
629. JESUS YOU DIED, TO MAKE ME HAPPY, I PRAISE YOU LORD JESUS, HALLELUJAH.
630. JESUS YOU DIED, TO GIVE ME HOPE, I PRAISE YOU LORD JESUS, HALLELUJAH.
631. JESUS YOU DIED, TO GIVE ME YOUR RIGHTEOUSNESS, I PRAISE YOU LORD JESUS, HALLELUJAH.
632. JESUS YOU DIED, FOR US TO BE TOGETHER, I PRAISE YOU LORD JESUS, HALLELUJAH.
633. JESUS YOU DIED, TO FREE ME FROM SIN, I PRAISE YOU LORD JESUS, HALLELUJAH.
634. JESUS YOU DIED, TO GIVE ME ETERNAL LIFE, I PRAISE YOU LORD JESUS, HALLELUJAH.
635. JESUS YOU DIED, FOR ME TO DEVELOP A RELATIONSHIP WITH YOU, I PRAISE YOU LORD JESUS, HALLELUJAH.
636. JESUS YOU DIED, FOR ME TO DEVELOP A RELATIONSHIP WITH FATHER GOD, I PRAISE YOU LORD JESUS, HALLELUJAH.
637. JESUS YOU DIED, FOR ME TO DEVELOP A RELATIONSHIP WITH THE HOLY SPIRIT, I PRAISE YOU LORD JESUS, HALLELUJAH.
638. JESUS YOU DIED, TO SHOW ME ALL THE SECRETS OF HEAVEN, I PRAISE YOU LORD JESUS, HALLELUJAH.
639. JESUS YOU DIED, FOR ME TO KNOW WHAT TRUE LOVE IS, I PRAISE YOU LORD JESUS, HALLELUJAH.

640. JESUS YOU DIED, SO I KNOW WHAT TRUE OBEDIENCE IS, I PRAISE YOU LORD JESUS, HALLELUJAH.

641. JESUS I AM YOUR AMBASSADOR FOR LIFE, I WILL WORSHIP YOU FOREVER, AMEN, I PRAISE YOU, HALLELUJAH

642. YOU ARE MY COUNSELOR JESUS I PRAISE YOU LORD, HALLELUJAH.

643. MY HELP COMES FROM THE LORD, THE MAKER OF HEAVEN AND EARTH, I WORSHIP YOU JESUS, HALLELUJAH.

644. GOD YOU SAID BLESSED IS HE WHO COMES IN THE NAME OF THE LORD, I WORSHIP YOU LORD JESUS, I PRAISE YOU LORD, HALLELUJAH.

645. I KNOW YOU ARE A SPIRIT LORD AND I WILL WORSHIP YOU IN SPIRIT AND IN TRUTH, HALLELUJAH, I PRAISE YOU GOD JESUS.

646. MY LORD JESUS YOU ARE THE PRINCE OF PEACE, I PRAISE YOU LORD AND MY GOD. HALLELUJAH.

647. IN YOUR PRESENCE I GIVE ALL CONTROL LORD JESUS, I PRAISE YOU, HALLELUJAH

648. I WILL STRETCH MY TIME WITH YOU LORD JESUS, I PRAISE YOU, HALLELUJAH.

649. I WILL STRETCH MY GIFTS AND UNDEFILED OFFERINGS TO JESUS, BECAUSE YOU LOVE ME, I PRAISE YOU JESUS, HALLELUJAH.

650. GOD YOU SAID BLESSED ARE THE POOR IN SPIRIT, FOR THEIRS IS THE KINGDOM OF HEAVEN, I PRAISE YOU JESUS, HALLELUJAH.

651. GOD YOU SAID BLESSED ARE THOSE WHO MOURN, FOR THEY WILL BE COMFORTED, I PRAISE YOU JESUS, HALLELUJAH.

652. GOD YOU SAID BLESSED ARE THE MEEK, FOR THEY WILL INHERIT THE EARTH, I PRAISE YOU JESUS, HALLELUJAH.

653. GOD YOU SAID BLESSED ARE THOSE WHO HUNGER AND THIRST FOR RIGHTEOUSNESS,

FOR THEY WILL BE FILLED, I PRAISE YOU JESUS, HALLELUJAH.

654. GOD YOU SAID BLESSED ARE THE MERCIFUL, FOR THEY WILL BE SHOWN MERCY, I PRAISE YOU JESUS, HALLELUJAH.

655. GOD YOU SAID BLESSED ARE THE PURE IN HEART, FOR THEY WILL SEE GOD, I PRAISE YOU JESUS, HALLELUJAH.

656. GOD YOU SAID BLESSED ARE THE PEACEMAKERS, FOR THEY WILL BE CALLED SONS OF GOD, I PRAISE YOU LORD JESUS, HALLELUJAH.

657. GOD YOU SAID BLESSED ARE THOSE WHO ARE PERSECUTED BECAUSE OF RIGHTEOUSNESS,

658. FOR THEIRS IS THE KINGDOM OF HEAVEN, I PRAISE YOU LORD JESUS, HALLELUJAH.

659. GOD YOU SAID BLESSED ARE YOU WHEN PEOPLE INSULT YOU, PERSECUTE YOU AND FALSELY SAY ALL KINDS OF EVIL AGAINST YOU BECAUSE OF ME, I PRAISE YOU

660. LORD JESUS, HALLELUJAH.

661. GOD YOU SAID REJOICE AND BE GLAD, BECAUSE GREAT IS MY REWARD IN HEAVEN, I PRAISE YOU LORD JESUS, HALLELUJAH.

662. I BELIEVE IN THE SON OF THE LIVING GOD, I PRAISE YOU JESUS. HALLELUJAH.

663. HOSANNA IN THE HIGHEST! I PRAISE YOU JESUS, HALLELUJAH.

664. HOSANNA IN THE HIGHEST! BLESSED IS HE WHO COMES IN THE NAME OF THE LORD!" I PRAISE YOU JESUS, HALLELUJAH.

665. HOSANNA TO THE SON OF DAVID. I PRAISE YOU JESUS, HALLELUJAH.

666. HOSANNA IN THE HIGHEST! I PRAISE YOU JESUS, HALLELUJAH.

667. HOSANNA IN THE HIGHEST! BLESSED IS HE WHO COMES IN THE NAME OF THE LORD! I PRAISE YOU JESUS, HALLELUJAH.

668. HOSANNA TO THE SON OF DAVID. I PRAISE YOU JESUS, HALLELUJAH.

669. GREAT IS YOUR MERCY LORD, I PRAISE YOU JESUS. HALLELUJAH.

670. HOLY HOLY HOLY IS THE LORD GOD ALMIGHTY JESUS CHRIST, I PRAISE YOU JESUS.

671. HOLY HOLY HOLY IS THE LORD GOD ALMIGHTY JESUS CHRIST, I PRAISE YOU JESUS.

672. HOLY HOLY HOLY IS THE LORD GOD ALMIGHTY JESUS CHRIST, I PRAISE YOU JESUS.

673. HOLY HOLY HOLY IS THE LORD GOD ALMIGHTY JESUS CHRIST, I PRAISE YOU JESUS.

674. HOLY HOLY HOLY IS THE LORD GOD ALMIGHTY JESUS CHRIST, I PRAISE YOU JESUS.

675. HOLY HOLY HOLY IS THE LORD GOD ALMIGHTY JESUS CHRIST, I PRAISE YOU JESUS.

676. HOLY HOLY HOLY IS THE LORD GOD ALMIGHTY JESUS CHRIST, I PRAISE YOU JESUS.

677. HALLELUJAH, HALLELUJAH, HALLELUJAH, I PRAISE YOU JESUS.

678. HALLELUJAH, HALLELUJAH, HALLELUJAH, I PRAISE YOU JESUS.

679. HALLELUJAH, HALLELUJAH, HALLELUJAH, I PRAISE YOU JESUS.

680. HALLELUJAH, HALLELUJAH, HALLELUJAH, I PRAISE YOU JESUS.

681. HALLELUJAH, HALLELUJAH, HALLELUJAH, I PRAISE YOU JESUS.

682. HALLELUJAH, HALLELUJAH, HALLELUJAH, I PRAISE YOU JESUS.

683. HALLELUJAH, HALLELUJAH, HALLELUJAH, I PRAISE YOU JESUS.

684. HAVE MERCY ON ME JESUS FOR I SIN AGAINST YOU, I PRAISE YOU. HALLELUJAH.

685. HAVE MERCY ON ME JESUS FOR I SIN AGAINST YOU, I PRAISE YOU. HALLELUJAH.

686. HAVE MERCY ON ME JESUS FOR I SIN AGAINST YOU, I PRAISE YOU. HALLELUJAH.

687. LORD GOD ALMIGHTY JESUS CHRIST, I PRAISE YOU.
688. LORD GOD ALMIGHTY JESUS CHRIST, I PRAISE YOU.
689. LORD GOD ALMIGHTY JESUS CHRIST, I PRAISE YOU.
690. I PRAISE YOU JESUS. HALLELUJAH.
691. I NEED YOU JESUS, TO SURVIVE. HALLELUJAH.
692. I LOVE YOU JESUS. HALLELUJAH.
693. YOU ARE IMPORTANT TO ME, JESUS. HALLELUJAH.
694. COME TO ME JESUS, HALLELUJAH.
695. LET ME FEEL YOU JESUS, HALLELUJAH.
696. I AM HAPPY TO BE PART OF YOUR BODY JESUS, I PRAISE YOU.
697. STAND WITH ME JESUS, HALLELUJAH.
698. YOU ARE GREAT JESUS, HALLELUJAH.
699. YOU ARE HOLY JESUS, HALLELUJAH.
700. YOU ARE FAITHFUL JESUS, HALLELUJAH.
701. JESUS YOU ARE LORD AND GOD, HALLELUJAH.
702. JESUS YOU ARE THE KING OF HEAVEN AND EARTH, I PRAISE YOU.
703. YOU ARE WONDERFUL JESUS, HALLELUJAH.
704. YOU ARE MARVELOUS JESUS, HALLELUJAH.
705. I CALL YOU RIGHTEOUS JESUS, HALLELUJAH.
706. I CALL YOU AWESOME JESUS, HALLELUJAH.
707. YOU ARE WORHTY OF ALL PRAISE JESUS, HALLELUJAH.
708. YOU ARE MERCIFUL JESUS, HALLELUJAH.
709. JESUS YOU ARE THE ALPHA AND OMEGA, I PRAISE YOU. HALLELUJAH.
710. YOU ARE THE PEACE MAKER JESUS, HALLELUJAH.
711. YOU ARE THE GLORIOUS JESUS, HALLELUJAH.
712. YOU ARE THE HEALER JESUS, HALLELUJAH.
713. YOU ARE THE LOVING JESUS, HALLELUJAH.
714. YOU ARE THE ROCK JESUS, HALLELUJAH.
715. COME AND HOLD ME JESUS, HALLELUJAH.

716. COME AND LOVE ME JESUS, HALLELUJAH.
717. I CAN'T DO WITHOUT YOU JESUS, HALLELUJAH.
718. SHOW YOURSELF TO ME JESUS, HALLELUJAH.
719. I WORSHIP YOU JESUS, HALLELUJAH.
720. I HONOR YOU JESUS, HALLELUJAH.
721. GREAT IS YOUR MERCY TOWARDS ME JESUS, HALLELUJAH.
722. YOU ARE THE GREAT PROVIDER JESUS, HALLELUJAH.
723. I THANK YOU FOR YOUR KINDNESS JESUS, HALLELUJAH.
724. THANKS FOR BEING MY SAVIOR JESUS, HALLELUJAH.
725. I PRAISE YOUR SPIRIT JESUS, HALLELUJAH.
726. I THANK YOU JESUS FOR GIVING ME ETERNAL LIFE, HALLELUJAH.
727. THANKS FOR BEING JUST TO ME JESUS, HALLELUJAH.
728. I THANK YOU JESUS FOR UNDERSTANDING MY NEEDS, I PRAISE YOU, HALLELUJAH.
729. I PRAISE YOU LORD GOD ALMIGHTY JESUS CHRIST, HALLELUJAH.
730. I PRAISE YOU LORD GOD ALMIGHTY JESUS CHRIST, HALLELUJAH.
731. I PRAISE YOU LORD GOD ALMIGHTY JESUS CHRIST, HALLELUJAH.
732. JESUS YOU ARE WORTHY OF ALL THE GLORY AND THE PRAISE, HALLELUJAH.
733. THERE IS NONE LIKE YOU LORD JESUS, HALLELUJAH.
734. YOU ARE HOLY LORD ALMIGHTY JESUS, HALLELUJAH.
735. YOU ARE HOLY LORD ALMIGHTY JESUS, HALLELUJAH.
736. YOU ARE HOLY LORD ALMIGHTY JESUS, HALLELUJAH.

737. YOU ARE THE LAMB ON THE THRONE JESUS, HALLELUJAH.
738. JESUS YOU ARE THE ONE AND ONLY SON OF GOD THE MOST HIGH, HALLELUJAH.
739. I WANT YOU TO TOUCH ME JESUS, HALLELUJAH.
740. I WANT YOU TO NEVER LEAVE ME JESUS, HALLELUJAH.
741. I WANT YOU ALWAYS IN MY LIFE LORD JESUS, HALLELUJAH.
742. I NEED YOU NOW LORD JESUS, I PRAISE YOU, HALLELUJAH.
743. JESUS YOU ARE THE KING OF KINGS, HALLELUJAH.
744. JESUS YOU ARE THE LORD OF LORDS, HALLELUJAH.
745. JESUS I KNOW YOU LIVE TODAY, I PRAISE YOU, HALLELUJAH.
746. JESUS I KNOW YOU WILL LIVE TOMORROW, I PRAISE YOU
747. JESUS THE GOD OF THE BIBLE IS GREAT AND GENEROUS, HALLELUJAH.
748. COME TO ME LORD JESUS LET ME SEE YOU, HALLELUJAH.
749. I WANT YOU TO HOLD ME LORD JESUS, HALLELUJAH.
750. I WANT TO FEEL YOUR LOVE LORD JESUS, HALLELUJAH.
751. JESUS YOU ARE THE CENTER OF MY JOY, I PRAISE YOU, HALLELUJAH.
752. HOLY HOLY HOLY IS THE LORD ALMIGHTY JESUS CHRIST, HALLELUJAH.
753. HOLY HOLY HOLY IS THE LORD ALMIGHTY JESUS CHRIST, HALLELUJAH.
754. HOLY HOLY HOLY IS THE LORD ALMIGHTY JESUS CHRIST, HALLELUJAH.
755. JESUS YOU ARE THE MAJOR PRESENCE IN MY LIFE, HALLELUJAH.

756. JESUS I NEED YOU NOW, HALLELUJAH.

757. JESUS COME RESCUE ME, HALLELUJAH.

758. JESUS DON'T WAIT ONE SECOND BEFORE YOU COME, HALLELUJAH.

759. JESUS I WANT TO SERVE YOU ALONE, HALLELUJAH.

760. LORD GOD ALMIGHTY JESUS CHRIST, I PRAISE YOU JESUS.

761. LORD GOD ALMIGHTY JESUS CHRIST, I PRAISE YOU JESUS.

762. LORD GOD ALMIGHTY JESUS CHRIST, I PRAISE YOU JESUS.

763. I HONOR YOU JESUS, I PRAISE YOU JESUS.

764. I WILL CONFORM TO YOUR BLESSED WAYS LORD JESUS, HALLELUJAH.

765. GREAT IS YOUR MERCY MY LORD JESUS, I PRAISE YOU JESUS.

766. JESUS YOU ARE EVER FAITHFUL, I PRAISE YOU JESUS.

767. DEAR JESUS YOU ARE THE GREAT I AM, I PRAISE YOU JESUS.

768. JESUS YOUR TENDER MERCY GIVE US ALL PEACE, I PRAISE YOU JESUS.

769. JESUS YOU ARE THE MIRACLE WORKER, I PRAISE YOU JESUS.

770. JESUS YOU ARE THE HEALER, I PRAISE YOU JESUS.

771. GREAT IS YOUR MERCY LORD, I PRAISE YOU JESUS

772. JESUS YOU DIED, TO SAVE ME, I WORSHIP YOU LORD JESUS.

773. JESUS YOU DIED, SO I AM HEALED, I WORSHIP YOU LORD JESUS.

774. JESUS YOU DIED, SO I OBTAIN GLORY, I WORSHIP YOU LORD JESUS.

775. JESUS YOU DIED, SO I OBTAIN LIFE, I WORSHIP YOU LORD JESUS.

776. JESUS YOU DIED, TO MAKE ME HAPPY, I WORSHIP YOU LORD JESUS.
777. JESUS YOU DIED, TO GIVE ME HOPE, I WORSHIP YOU LORD JESUS.
778. JESUS YOU DIED, TO GIVE ME YOUR RIGHTEOUSNESS, I WORSHIP YOU LORD JESUS.
779. JESUS YOU DIED, FOR US TO BE TOGETHER, I WORSHIP YOU LORD JESUS.
780. JESUS YOU DIED, TO FREE ME FROM SIN, I WORSHIP YOU LORD JESUS.
781. JESUS YOU DIED, TO GIVE ME ETERNAL LIFE, I WORSHIP YOU LORD JESUS.
782. JESUS YOU DIED, TO PROSPER ME, I WORSHIP YOU LORD JESUS.
783. JESUS YOU DIED, FOR ME TO DEVELOP A RELATIONSHIP WITH YOU, I WORSHIP YOU LORD JESUS.
784. JESUS YOU DIED, FOR ME TO DEVELOP A RELATIONSHIP WITH OUR FATHER GOD, I WORSHIP YOU LORD JESUS.
785. JESUS YOU DIED, FOR ME TO HAVE A RELATIONSHIP WITH THE HOLY SPIRIT, I WORSHIP YOU LORD JESUS.
786. JESUS YOU DIED, TO SHOW ME ALL THE SECRETS OF HEAVEN, I WORSHIP YOU LORD JESUS.
787. JESUS YOU DIED, FOR ME TO KNOW WHAT TRUE LOVE IS, I WORSHIP YOU LORD JESUS.
788. JESUS YOU DIED, SO I KNOW WHAT TRUE OBEDIENCE IS, I WORSHIP YOU LORD JESUS.
789. JESUS I KNOW YOU LIVE TODAY, I PRAISE YOU LORD JESUS.
790. THERE IS NO GOD LIKE YOU JESUS, I PRAISE YOU LORD JESUS.
791. PURIFY ME JESUS, I PRAISE YOU LORD JESUS.
792. MAKE YOURSELF KNOWN TO ME JESUS, I PRAISE YOU LORD JESUS.

793. JESUS YOUR HEART IS CLEAN AND JUST, I PRAISE YOU LORD JESUS.

794. WHEN I CALL YOUR NAME JESUS YOU NEVER SAY NO, I PRAISE YOU LORD JESUS.

795. YOU HAVE PROMISED TO BLESS ME IF I OBEY YOU, I PRAISE YOU LORD JESUS JESUS.

796. YOU HAVE PROMISED TO COME NEAR ME IF I COME NEAR YOU, I PRAISE YOU LORD JESUS.

797. YOU HAVE PROMISED TO WATCH OVER AND COUNSEL ME, I PRAISE YOU LORD JESUS.

798. YOU PROMISED NOT A HAIR ON MY HEAD WILL PERISH, I PRAISE YOU LORD JESUS.

799. YOU PROMISED, IF I CALL ON YOU IN TIMES OF TROUBLE; YOU WILL DELIVER ME AND HONOR ME, I PRAISE YOU LORD JESUS.

800. YOU PROMISED TO NEVER FORSAKE ME OR LEAVE ME, I PRAISE YOU LORD JESUS.

801. YOU PROMISED THAT IF I CONFESS MY SINS, YOU WILL BE FAITHFUL AND JUST TO ME, AND YOU WILL FORGIVE ME OF MY SINS AND PURIFY ME FROM ALL UNRIGHTEOUSNESS, I PRAISE YOU LORD JESUS.

802. ONLY YOU ARE HOLY JESUS, I WORSHIP YOU LORD JESUS.

803. ONLY YOU ARE HOLY JESUS, I WORSHIP YOU LORD JESUS.

804. ONLY YOU ARE HOLY JESUS, I WORSHIP YOU LORD JESUS.

805. THE SPIRIT OF GOD IS ON YOU JESUS, I PRAISE YOU LORD JESUS.

806. GOD THE FATHER HAS ANOINTED YOU JESUS, I PRAISE YOU LORD. HALLELUJAH.

807. JESUS YOU PREACH GOOD NEWS TO THE POOR, I PRAISE YOU LORD. HALLELUJAH.

808. JESUS YOU CAME TO PROCLAIM FREEDOM FOR THE PRISONERS, I PRAISE YOU LORD JESUS.

809. RECOVERY OF SIGHT FOR THE BLIND, YOU PROVIDED JESUS, I PRAISE YOU LORD JESUS.

810. JESUS, YOU RELEASED THE OPPRESSED, I PRAISE YOU LORD JESUS, HALLELUJAH.

811. JESUS YOU PROCLAIM THE YEAR OF THE LORD'S FAVOR, I PRAISE YOU LORD JESUS, HALLELUJAH.

812. YOUR GREATEST PLEASURE JESUS IS FOR US TO BELIEVE YOU, I BELIEVE YOU AND WORSHIP YOU LORD JESUS, HALLELUJAH.

813. I DO NOT DOUBT YOU JESUS, I PRAISE YOU LORD JESUS, HALLELUJAH.

814. MY LORD JESUS YOU ARE THE GREAT LION OF JUDAH, HALLELUJAH.

815. OH JESUS HOW POWERFUL YOU ARE, I PRAISE YOU JESUS, HALLELUJAH.

816. YOU ARE HOLY, LORD JESUS, I PRAISE YOU LORD JESUS, HALLELUJAH.

817. YOU ARE HOLY, LORD JESUS, I PRAISE YOU LORD JESUS, HALLELUJAH.

818. YOU ARE HOLY, MY JESUS , I PRAISE YOU LORD JESUS, HALLELUJAH.

819. JESUS YOU ARE THE SUN OF MAN, I PRAISE YOU LORD JESUS, HALLELUJAH.

820. MY LOVING JESUS BE WITH ME LORD JESUS, I PRAISE YOU JESUS, HALLELUJAH.

821. STAY WITH ME LORD JESUS, HALLELUJAH.

822. NEVER LEAVE ME LORD JESUS, HALLELUJAH.

823. I HAVE TO HAVE YOU WITH ME LORD JESUS, HALLELUJAH.

824. I WANT YOU LORD JESUS, I PRAISE YOU JESUS, HALLELUJAH.

825. I LOVE YOU LORD JESUS, I PRAISE YOU JESUS, HALLELUJAH.

826. I WANT YOUR INTENSE LOVE LORD JESUS, HALLELUJAH.

827. SHOW YOURSELF TO ME, LOVING JESUS, HALLELUJAH.

828. YOU MADE THE HEAVENS AND THE EARTH, I WORSHIP YOU JESUS, HALLELUJAH.

829. MY KING IS MY GREATEST POSSESSION, I WORSHIP YOU JESUS, HALLELUJAH.
830. MY REDEEMER FROM EVERLASTING IS YOUR NAME JESUS, HALLELUJAH.
831. YOU ARE AWESOME, YOU ARE AWESOME OUR GOD JESUS, HALLELUJAH.
832. I LOVE YOU JESUS FOREVER, HALLELUJAH.
833. I LIFT MY HANDS UP TO YOU JESUS, I PRAISE YOU, HALLELUJAH.
834. MELODIES FROM HEAVEN RAIN DOWN ON ME, I PRAISE YOU JESUS, HALLELUJAH.
835. GIVE ME ALL YOUR JOY LORD, I PRAISE YOU JESUS HALLELUJAH.
836. THANKS FOR YOUR PEACE, I WORSHIP YOU JESUS HALLELUJAH.
837. I THANK YOU FOR THE HOLY SPIRIT, I WORSHIP YOU JESUS, HALLELUJAH.
838. I THANK YOU FOR YOUR BLESSINGS LORD, I WORSHIP YOU JESUS, HALLELUJAH.
839. I THANK YOU FOR GIVING ME UNDERSTANDING LORD, I WORSHIP YOU JESUS, HALLELUJAH.
840. I THANK YOU FOR WISDOM, I WORSHIP YOU JESUS, HALLELUJAH.
841. I THANK YOU FOR LONG LIFE, I WORSHIP YOU JESUS, HALLELUJAH.
842. I THANK YOU FOR GREAT HEALTH, I WORSHIP YOU JESUS, HALLELUJAH.
843. I THANK YOU FOR CHOSING ME FOR SALVATION, I WORSHIP YOU JESUS, HALLELUJAH.
844. YOUR LOVE IS EVERLASTING LORD, I WORSHIP YOU JESUS, HALLELUJAH.
845. NO ONE CAN LOVE ME LIKE YOU LORD, I PRAISE YOU JESUS, HALLELUJAH.
846. NO ONE KNOWS ME LIKE YOU DO, I PRAISE YOU JESUS, HALLELUJAH.
847. YOU ARE ALWAYS IN MY LIFE LORD, I PRAISE YOU JESUS, HALLELUJAH.

848. YOU ARE ALWAYS GIVING ME A LIFE LINE LORD, I PRAISE YOU JESUS, HALLELUJAH.
849. I WILL PRAISE YOU JESUS FOREVER, HALLELUJAH.
850. THE SWORD OF THE SPIRIT COMES FROM YOU JESUS, I PRAISE YOU, HALLELUJAH.
851. JESUS YOU ARE THE GREAT 'I AM' OF THE OLD SCRIPTURES, I WORSHIP YOU, HALLELUJAH.
852. THERE IS NOTHING MAN CAN DO TO SEPARATE US LORD, I PRAISE YOU JESUS, HALLELUJAH.
853. SHOW ME THE WAY LORD, I PRAISE YOU JESUS, HALLELUJAH.
854. HELP ME LORD, I PRAISE YOU JESUS, HALLELUJAH.
855. ALL THINGS ARE POSSIBLE LORD, I PRAISE YOU JESUS, HALLELUJAH.
856. LORD YOU ARE ABLE TO DO ALL THINGS, I PRAISE YOU JESUS, HALLELUJAH.
857. I FALL DOWN LORD BUT I GET UP IN YOUR POWER, I PRAISE YOU JESUS, HALLELUJAH.
858. GREAT IS YOUR MERCY LORD, I WORSHIP YOU, JESUS.
859. I BELIEVE IN THE BODY OF THE LORD, I PRAISE YOU JESUS, HALLELUJAH.
860. I BELIEVE IN THE WORSHIP OF THE LORD, I PRAISE YOU JESUS, HALLELUJAH.
861. I BELIEVE IN THE BLOOD OF THE LORD, I PRAISE YOU JESUS, HALLELUJAH.
862. I BELIEVE IN THE LIFE OF THE LORD, I PRAISE YOU JESUS, HALLELUJAH.
863. I BELIEVE IN THE SPIRIT OF THE LORD, I PRAISE YOU JESUS, HALLELUJAH.
864. I BELIEVE IN THE HEART OF THE LORD, I PRAISE YOU JESUS, HALLELUJAH.
865. I BELIEVE IN THE FATHER OF THE LORD, I PRAISE YOU JESUS, HALLELUJAH.
866. I BELIEVE IN THE WILL OF THE LORD, I PRAISE YOU JESUS, HALLELUJAH.

867. I BELIEVE IN THE AUTHORITY OF THE LORD, I PRAISE YOU JESUS, HALLELUJAH.

868. I BELIEVE IN THE LOVE OF THE LORD, I PRAISE YOU JESUS, HALLELUJAH.

869. I BELIEVE IN THE GRACE OF THE LORD, I PRAISE YOU JESUS, HALLELUJAH.

870. I BELIEVE IN THE JOY OF THE LORD, I PRAISE YOU JESUS, HALLELUJAH.

871. I BELIEVE IN THE INSPIRATION OF THE LORD, I PRAISE YOU JESUS, HALLELUJAH.

872. I BELIEVE IN THE LIGHT OF THE LORD, I PRAISE YOU JESUS, HALLELUJAH.

873. I BELIEVE IN THE FAITH OF THE LORD, I PRAISE YOU JESUS, HALLELUJAH.

874. I BELIEVE IN THE UNDERSTANDING OF THE LORD, I PRAISE YOU JESUS, HALLELUJAH.

875. I BELIEVE IN THE PRAISES OF THE LORD, I PRAISE YOU JESUS, HALLELUJAH.

876. I BELIEVE IN THE SONG OF THE LORD, I PRAISE YOU JESUS, HALLELUJAH.

877. I BELIEVE IN THE SON OF THE LIVING GOD, I PRAISE YOU JESUS, HALLELUJAH.

878. I BELIEVE IN THE BLESSINGS OF THE LORD, I PRAISE YOU JESUS, HALLELUJAH.

879. YOUR GREATEST ACT LORD WAS TO DECIEVE THE GREAT DECIEVER, I PRAISE YOU JESUS, HALLELUJAH.

880. HAVE MERCY ON ME JESUS FOR I SIN AGAINST YOU ALONE, I PRAISE YOU ALONE, HALLELUJAH.

881. HAVE MERCY ON ME JESUS FOR I SIN AGAINST YOU ALONE, I PRAISE YOU ALONE, HALLELUJAH.

882. HAVE MERCY ON ME JESUS FOR I SIN AGAINST YOU ALONE, I PRAISE YOU ALONE, HALLELUJAH.

883. HALLELUJAH, HALLELUJAH, HALLELUJAH, JESUS.

884. LORD GOD ALMIGHTY JESUS CHRIST, I PRAISE YOU, HALLELUJAH.
885. HALLELUJAH, HALLELUJAH, HALLELUJAH, JESUS.
886. LORD GOD ALMIGHTY JESUS CHRIST, I PRAISE YOU, HALLELUJAH.
887. HALLELUJAH, HALLELUJAH, HALLELUJAH, JESUS.
888. LORD GOD ALMIGHTY JESUS CHRIST, I PRAISE YOU, HALLELUJAH.
889. I PRAISE YOU JESUS, HALLELUJAH.
890. I NEED YOU JESUS TO SURVIVE LORD, HALLELUJAH.
891. I LOVE YOU JESUS, HALLELUJAH.
892. YOU ARE IMPORTANT TO ME JESUS, HALLELUJAH.
893. COME TO ME JESUS, HALLELUJAH.
894. LET ME FEEL YOU JESUS, HALLELUJAH.
895. I AM HAPPY TO BE PART OF YOUR BODY JESUS, I PRAISE YOU, HALLELUJAH.
896. STAND WITH ME JESUS, HALLELUJAH.
897. YOU ARE GREAT JESUS, HALLELUJAH.
898. YOU ARE HOLY JESUS, HALLELUJAH.
899. YOU ARE FAITHFUL JESUS, HALLELUJAH.
900. JESUS YOU ARE MY LORD AND MY GOD, HALLELUJAH.
901. JESUS YOU ARE THE KING OF HEAVEN AND EARTH, I PRAISE YOU, HALLELUJAH.
902. YOU ARE WONDERFUL JESUS, HALLELUJAH.
903. YOU ARE MARVELOUS JESUS, HALLELUJAH.
904. I CALL YOU RIGHTEOUS JESUS, HALLELUJAH.
905. I CALL YOU AWESOME JESUS, HALLELUJAH.
906. YOU ARE WORHTY OF ALL PRAISE JESUS, HALLELUJAH.
907. YOU ARE MERCIFUL JESUS, HALLELUJAH.
908. JESUS YOU ARE THE ALPHA AND OMEGA, I PRAISE YOU, HALLELUJAH.

909. YOU ARE THE PEACE MAKER JESUS, HALLELUJAH.
910. YOU ARE THE GLORIOUS JESUS, HALLELUJAH.
911. YOU ARE THE HEALER JESUS, HALLELUJAH.
912. YOU ARE THE LOVING JESUS, HALLELUJAH.
913. YOU ARE THE ROCK JESUS, HALLELUJAH.
914. COME AND HOLD ME JESUS, HALLELUJAH.
915. COME AND LOVE ME JESUS, HALLELUJAH.
916. I CAN'T DO WITHOUT YOU JESUS, HALLELUJAH.
917. SHOW YOURSELF TO ME JESUS, HALLELUJAH.
918. I WORSHIP YOU JESUS, HALLELUJAH.
919. I HONOR YOU JESUS, HALLELUJAH.
920. GREAT IS YOUR MERCY TOWARDS ME JESUS, HALLELUJAH.
921. YOU ARE THE GREAT PROVIDER JESUS, HALLELUJAH.
922. I THANK YOU FOR YOUR KINDNESS JESUS, HALLELUJAH.
923. THANKS FOR BEING MY SAVIOR JESUS, HALLELUJAH.
924. I PRAISE YOUR SPIRIT JESUS, HALLELUJAH.
925. I THANK YOU JESUS FOR GIVING ME ETERNAL LIFE, HALLELUJAH.
926. THANKS FOR BEING JUST TO ME JESUS, HALLELUJAH.
927. I THANK YOU JESUS FOR UNDERSTANDING MY NEEDS, I PRAISE YOU, HALLELUJAH.
928. I PRAISE YOU LORD GOD ALMIGHTY JESUS CHRIST, HALLELUJAH.
929. I PRAISE YOU LORD GOD ALMIGHTY JESUS CHRIST, HALLELUJAH.
930. I PRAISE YOU LORD GOD ALMIGHTY JESUS CHRIST, HALLELUJAH.
931. JESUS YOU ARE WORTHY OF ALL THE GLORY AND ALL THE PRAISE, HALLELUJAH.
932. THERE IS NONE LIKE YOU LORD JESUS, HALLELUJAH.

933. YOU ARE HOLY LORD GOD ALMIGHTY JESUS CHRIST, HALLELUJAH.

934. YOU ARE HOLY LORD GOD ALMIGHTY JESUS CHRIST, HALLELUJAH.

935. YOU ARE HOLY LORD GOD ALMIGHTY JESUS CHRIST, HALLELUJAH.

936. YOU ARE THE LAMB ON THE THRONE JESUS, HALLELUJAH.

937. JESUS YOU ARE THE ONE AND ONLY SON OF GOD THE MOST HIGH, HALLELUJAH.

938. I WANT YOU TO TOUCH ME JESUS, HALLELUJAH.

939. I WANT YOU TO NEVER LEAVE ME JESUS, HALLELUJAH.

940. I WANT YOU TO ALWAYS BE IN MY LIFE LORD JESUS, HALLELUJAH.

941. I NEED YOU NOW LORD JESUS, I PRAISE YOU JESUS, HALLELUJAH.

942. JESUS YOU ARE THE KING OF KINGS, HALLELUJAH.

943. JESUS YOU ARE THE LORD OF LORDS, HALLELUJAH.

944. JESUS I KNOW YOU LIVE TODAY, I PRAISE YOU JESUS, HALLELUJAH.

945. JESUS I KNOW YOU WILL LIVE TOMORROW, I PRAISE YOU JESUS, HALLELUJAH.

946. JESUS THE GOD OF THE BIBLE IS GREAT AND GENEROUS, HALLELUJAH.

947. COME TO ME LORD JESUS LET ME SEE YOU, HALLELUJAH.

948. I WANT YOU TO HOLD ME LORD JESUS, HALLELUJAH.

949. I WANT TO FEEL YOUR LOVE LORD JESUS, HALLELUJAH.

950. JESUS YOU ARE THE CENTER OF MY JOY, I PRAISE YOU, HALLELUJAH.

951. HOLY HOLY HOLY IS THE LORD ALMIGHTY JESUS CHRIST, HALLELUJAH.

952. HOLY HOLY HOLY IS THE LORD ALMIGHTY JESUS CHRIST, HALLELUJAH.

953. HOLY HOLY HOLY IS THE LORD ALMIGHTY JESUS CHRIST, HALLELUJAH.

954. JESUS YOU ARE THE MAJOR PRESENCE IN MY LIFE, HALLELUJAH.

955. JESUS I NEED YOU NOW, HALLELUJAH.

956. JESUS COME RESCUE ME, HALLELUJAH.

957. JESUS DON'T WAIT ONE SECOND BEFORE YOU COME, HALLELUJAH.

958. JESUS I WANT TO SERVE YOU ALONE, HALLELUJAH.

959. HALLELUJAH, HALLELUJAH, HALLELUJAH, JESUS.

960. LORD GOD ALMIGHTY JESUS CHRIST, I PRAISE YOU, HALLELUJAH.

961. HALLELUJAH, HALLELUJAH, HALLELUJAH, JESUS.

962. LORD GOD ALMIGHTY JESUS CHRIST, I PRAISE YOU, HALLELUJAH.

963. HALLELUJAH, HALLELUJAH, HALLELUJAH, JESUS.

964. LORD GOD ALMIGHTY JESUS CHRIST, I PRAISE YOU JESUS, HALLELUJAH.

965. I HONOR YOU JESUS, I PRAISE YOU, HALLELUJAH.

966. I WILL CONFORM TO YOUR BLESSED WAYS LORD JESUS, HALLELUJAH.

967. GREAT IS YOUR WILL AND YOUR MERCY MY LORD JESUS, I PRAISE YOU JESUS, HALLELUJAH.

968. JESUS YOU ARE EVER FAITHFUL, I PRAISE YOU JESUS, HALLELUJAH.

969. DEAR JESUS YOU ARE THE GREAT I AM, I PRAISE YOU JESUS, HALLELUJAH.

970. JESUS YOUR TENDER MERCY GIVE US ALL PEACE, I PRAISE YOU JESUS, HALLELUJAH.

971. JESUS YOU ARE THE MIRACLE WORKER, I PRAISE YOU JESUS, HALLELUJAH.
972. JESUS YOU ARE THE HEALER, I PRAISE YOU JESUS, HALLELUJAH.
973. HOSANNA IN THE HIGHEST! I PRAISE YOU JESUS, HALLELUJAH.
974. HOSANNA IN THE HIGHEST! BLESSED IS HE WHO COMES IN THE NAME OF THE LORD! I PRAISE YOU JESUS, HALLELUJAH.
975. HOSANNA TO THE SON OF DAVID. I PRAISE YOU JESUS, HALLELUJAH.
976. JESUS YOU DIED, TO SAVE ME, I PRAISE YOU JESUS, HALLELUJAH.
977. JESUS YOU DIED, SO I AM HEALED, I PRAISE YOU JESUS, HALLELUJAH.
978. JESUS YOU DIED, SO I OBTAIN GLORY, I PRAISE YOU JESUS, HALLELUJAH.
979. JESUS YOU DIED, SO I OBTAIN LIFE, I PRAISE YOU JESUS, HALLELUJAH.
980. JESUS YOU DIED, TO MAKE ME HAPPY, I PRAISE YOU JESUS, HALLELUJAH.
981. JESUS YOU DIED, TO GIVE ME HOPE, I PRAISE YOU JESUS, HALLELUJAH.
982. JESUS YOU DIED, TO GIVE ME YOUR RIGHTEOUSNESS, I PRAISE YOU JESUS, HALLELUJAH.
983. JESUS YOU DIED, FOR US TO BE TOGETHER, I PRAISE YOU JESUS, HALLELUJAH.
984. JESUS YOU DIED, TO FREE ME FROM SIN, I PRAISE YOU JESUS, HALLELUJAH.
985. JESUS YOU DIED, TO GIVE ME ETERNAL LIFE, I PRAISE YOU JESUS, HALLELUJAH.
986. JESUS YOU DIED, TO PROSPER ME, I PRAISE YOU, HALLELUJAH.
987. JESUS YOU DIED, FOR ME TO DEVELOP A RELATIONSHIP WITH YOU, I PRAISE YOU JESUS, HALLELUJAH.

988. JESUS YOU DIED, FOR ME TO DEVELOP A RELATIONSHIP WITH OUR FATHER GOD, I PRAISE YOU JESUS, HALLELUJAH.

989. JESUS YOU DIED, FOR ME TO HAVE A RELATIONSHIP WITH THE HOLY SPIRIT, I PRAISE YOU JESUS, HALLELUJAH.

990. JESUS YOU DIED, TO SHOW ME ALL THE SECRETS OF HEAVEN, I PRAISE YOU JESUS, HALLELUJAH.

991. JESUS YOU DIED, FOR ME TO KNOW WHAT TRUE LOVE IS, I PRAISE YOU JESUS, HALLELUJAH.

992. JESUS YOU DIED, SO I KNOW WHAT TRUE OBEDIENCE IS, I PRAISE YOU JESUS, HALLELUJAH.

993. JESUS I KNOW YOU LIVE TODAY, I PRAISE YOU JESUS, HALLELUJAH.

994. THERE IS NO GOD LIKE YOU JESUS, I PRAISE YOU JESUS, HALLELUJAH.

995. PURIFY ME JESUS, I PRAISE YOU JESUS, HALLELUJAH.

996. MAKE YOURSELF KNOWN TO ME JESUS, I PRAISE YOU JESUS, HALLELUJAH.

997. JESUS YOUR HEART IS CLEAN AND JUST, I PRAISE YOU JESUS, HALLELUJAH.

998. WHEN I CALL YOUR NAME JESUS YOU NEVER SAY NO, I PRAISE YOU JESUS, HALLELUJAH.

999. YOU HAVE PROMISED TO BLESS ME IF I OBEY YOU, I PRAISE YOU LORD JESUS, HALLELUJAH.

1000. YOU HAVE PROMISED TO COME NEAR ME IF I COME NEAR YOU, I PRAISE YOU LORD JESUS, HALLELUJAH.

1001. YOU HAVE PROMISED TO WATCH OVER AND COUNSEL ME, I PRAISE YOU LORD JESUS, HALLELUJAH.

1002. YOU PROMISED NOT A HAIR ON MY HEAD WILL PERISH, I PRAISE YOU LORD JESUS, HALLELUJAH.

1003. YOU PROMISED, IF I CALL ON YOU IN TIMES OF TROUBLE; YOU WILL DELIVER ME AND HONOR ME, I PRAISE YOU LORD JESUS, HALLELUJAH.

1004. YOU PROMISED TO NEVER FORSAKE ME OR LEAVE ME, I PRAISE YOU LORD JESUS, HALLELUJAH.

1005. YOU PROMISED THAT IF I CONFESS MY SINS, YOU WILL BE FAITHFUL AND JUST TO ME, AND YOU WILL FORGIVE ME OF MY SINS AND PURIFY ME FROM ALL UNRIGHTEOUSNESS, I PRAISE YOU LORD JESUS, HALLELUJAH.

1006. ONLY YOU ARE HOLY JESUS, I PRAISE YOU LORD JESUS, HALLELUJAH.

1007. ONLY YOU ARE HOLY JESUS, I PRAISE YOU LORD JESUS, HALLELUJAH.

1008. ONLY YOU ARE HOLY JESUS, I PRAISE YOU LORD JESUS, HALLELUJAH.

1009. THE SPIRIT OF GOD IS ON YOU JESUS, I PRAISE YOU LORD JESUS, HALLELUJAH.

1010. GOD THE FATHER HAS ANOINTED YOU JESUS, I PRAISE YOU LORD JESUS, HALLELUJAH.

1011. JESUS YOU PREACH GOOD NEWS TO THE POOR, I PRAISE YOU LORD JESUS, HALLELUJAH.

1012. JESUS YOU CAME TO PROCLAIM FREEDOM FOR THE PRISONERS, I PRAISE YOU LORD JESUS, HALLELUJAH.

1013. RECOVERY OF SIGHT FOR THE BLIND, YOU PROVIDED JESUS, I PRAISE YOU LORD JESUS, HALLELUJAH.

1014. YOU RAISED THE DEAD LORD JESUS, I WORSHIP YOU JESUS, HALLELUJAH.

1015. JESUS, YOU RELEASED THE OPPRESSED, I PRAISE YOU LORD JESUS, HALLELUJAH.

1016. JESUS YOU PROCLAIM THE YEAR OF THE LORD'S FAVOR, I PRAISE YOU LORD JESUS, HALLELUJAH.

1017. YOUR GREATEST PLEASURE JESUS IS FOR US TO BELIEVE YOU, I BELIEVE YOU AND PRAISE YOU LORD JESUS, HALLELUJAH.
1018. I DO NOT DOUBT YOU JESUS, I PRAISE YOU LORD JESUS, HALLELUJAH.
1019. MY LORD JESUS YOU ARE THE GREAT LION OF JUDAH, HALLELUJAH.
1020. OH JESUS HOW POWERFUL YOU ARE, I PRAISE YOU JESUS, HALLELUJAH.
1021. YOU ARE HOLY, LORD JESUS, I PRAISE YOUR HOLY NAME, HALLELUJAH.
1022. YOU ARE HOLY, LORD JESUS, I PRAISE YOUR HOLY NAME, HALLELUJAH.
1023. YOU ARE HOLY, OUR GOD JESUS, I PRAISE YOUR HOLY NAME, HALLELUJAH.
1024. JESUS YOU ARE THE SUN OF MAN, I PRAISE YOUR HOLY NAME, HALLELUJAH.
1025. MY LOVING JESUS BE WITH ME LORD JESUS, I PRAISE YOUR HOLY NAME, HALLELUJAH.
1026. STAY WITH ME LORD JESUS, HALLELUJAH.
1027. NEVER LEAVE ME LORD JESUS, HALLELUJAH.
1028. I HAVE TO HAVE YOU WITH ME LORD JESUS, HALLELUJAH.
1029. I WANT YOU WITH ME LORD JESUS, I PRAISE YOUR HOLY NAME, HALLELUJAH.
1030. I LOVE YOU LORD JESUS, I PRAISE YOUR HOLY NAME, HALLELUJAH.
1031. I WANT YOUR INTENSE LOVE, LORD JESUS, HALLELUJAH.
1032. SHOW YOURSELF TO ME LOVING JESUS, HALLELUJAH.
1033. YOU MADE THE HEAVENS AND THE EARTH, I PRAISE YOUR HOLY NAME JESUS, HALLELUJAH.
1034. MY KING IS MY GREATEST POSSESSION, I PRAISE YOU JESUS, HALLELUJAH.
1035. MY REDEEMER FROM EVERLASTING IS YOUR NAME JESUS, HALLELUJAH.

1036. YOU ARE AWESOME, YOU ARE AWESOME MY GOD AND LORD JESUS, HALLELUJAH .

1037. I LOVE YOU JESUS, HALLELUJAH.

1038. I LIFT MY HANDS UP TO YOU JESUS, I PRAISE YOU, HALLELUJAH.

1039. MELODIES FROM HEAVEN RAIN DOWN ON ME, I PRAISE YOUR HOLY NAME JESUS, HALLELUJAH.

1040. GIVE ME ALL YOUR JOY LORD, I PRAISE YOU JESUS, HALLELUJAH.

1041. THANKS FOR YOUR PEACE, I PRAISE YOU JESUS, HALLELUJAH.

1042. I THANK YOU FOR THE HOLY SPIRIT, I PRAISE YOU JESUS, HALLELUJAH.

1043. I THANK YOU FOR YOUR BLESSINGS LORD, I PRAISE YOU JESUS, HALLELUJAH.

1044. I THANK FOR GIVING ME UNDERSTANDING, I PRAISE YOU JESUS, HALLELUJAH.

1045. I THANK YOU FOR WISDOM, I PRAISE YOU JESUS, HALLELUJAH.

1046. I THANK YOU FOR LONG LIFE, I PRAISE YOU JESUS, HALLELUJAH.

1047. I THANK YOU FOR GREAT HEALTH, I PRAISE YOU JESUS, HALLELUJAH.

1048. I THANK YOU FOR CHOSING ME FOR SALVATION, I PRAISE YOU JESUS, HALLELUJAH.

1049. YOUR LOVE IS EVERLASTING, I PRAISE YOU JESUS, HALLELUJAH.

1050. NO ONE CAN LOVE ME LIKE YOU LORD, I PRAISE YOU JESUS, HALLELUJAH.

1051. NO ONE KNOWS ME LIKE YOU, I PRAISE YOU JESUS, HALLELUJAH.

1052. YOU ARE ALWAYS IN MY LIFE LORD, I PRAISE YOU JESUS, HALLELUJAH.

1053. YOU ARE ALWAYS GIVING ME A LIFE LINE LORD, I PRAISE YOU JESUS, HALLELUJAH.

1054. I WILL PRAISE YOU JESUS FOREVER, HALLELUJAH.

1055. THE SWORD OF THE SPIRIT COMES FROM YOU JESUS, I PRAISE YOU, HALLELUJAH.

1056. JESUS YOU ARE THE GREAT 'I AM' OF THE OLD SCRIPTURES, I PRAISE YOU, HALLELUJAH .

1057. THERE IS NOTHING MAN CAN DO TO SEPARATE US, I PRAISE YOU JESUS, HALLELUJAH.

1058. SHOW ME THE WAY LORD, I PRAISE YOU JESUS, HALLELUJAH.

1059. HELP ME LORD, I PRAISE YOU JESUS, HALLELUJAH.

1060. ALL THINGS ARE POSSIBLE LORD, I PRAISE YOU JESUS, HALLELUJAH.

1061. LORD YOU ARE ABLE, I PRAISE YOU JESUS, HALLELUJAH.

1062. WE FALL DOWN LORD BUT WE GET UP WITH YOUR POWER LORD, I PRAISE YOU JESUS, HALLELUJAH.

1063. I BELIEVE IN THE BODY OF THE LORD, I PRAISE YOU JESUS, HALLELUJAH.

1064. I BELIEVE IN THE WORSHIP OF THE LORD, I PRAISE YOU JESUS, HALLELUJAH.

1065. I BELIEVE IN THE BLOOD OF THE LORD, I PRAISE YOU JESUS, HALLELUJAH.

1066. I BELIEVE IN THE LIFE OF THE LORD, I PRAISE YOU JESUS, HALLELUJAH.

1067. I BELIEVE IN THE SPIRIT OF THE LORD, I PRAISE YOU JESUS, HALLELUJAH.

1068. I BELIEVE IN THE HEART OF THE LORD, I PRAISE YOU JESUS, HALLELUJAH.

1069. I BELIEVE IN THE FATHER OF THE LORD, I PRAISE YOU JESUS, HALLELUJAH.

1070. I BELIEVE IN THE WILL OF THE LORD, I PRAISE YOU JESUS, HALLELUJAH.

1071. I BELIEVE IN THE AUTHORITY OF THE LORD, I PRAISE YOU JESUS, HALLELUJAH.

1072. I BELIEVE IN THE LOVE OF THE LORD, I PRAISE YOU JESUS, HALLELUJAH.

1073. I BELIEVE IN THE GRACE OF THE LORD, I PRAISE YOU JESUS, HALLELUJAH.

1074. I BELIEVE IN THE JOY OF THE LORD, I PRAISE YOU JESUS, HALLELUJAH.

1075. I BELIEVE IN THE INSPIRATION OF THE LORD, I PRAISE YOU JESUS, HALLELUJAH.

1076. I BELIEVE IN THE LIGHT OF THE LORD, I PRAISE YOU JESUS, HALLELUJAH.

1077. I BELIEVE IN THE FAITH OF THE LORD, I PRAISE YOU JESUS, HALLELUJAH.

1078. I BELIEVE IN THE UNDERSTANDING OF THE LORD, I PRAISE YOU JESUS HALLELUJAH.

1079. I BELIEVE IN THE PRAISES OF THE LORD, I PRAISE YOU JESUS HALLELUJAH.

1080. I BELIEVE IN THE SONG OF THE LORD, I PRAISE YOU JESUS, HALLELUJAH.

1081. I BELIEVE IN THE SON OF THE LIVING GOD, I PRAISE YOU JESUS HALLELUJAH.

1082. I BELIEVE IN THE BLESSINGS OF THE LORD, I PRAISE YOU JESUS HALLELUJAH.

1083. I BELIEVE IN THE OBEDIENCE OF THE LORD, I PRAISE YOU JESUS HALLELUJAH.

1084. HOSANNA IN THE HIGHEST! I PRAISE YOU JESUS, HALLELUJAH.

1085. HOSANNA IN THE HIGHEST! BLESSED IS HE WHO COMES IN THE NAME OF THE LORD! I PRAISE YOU JESUS, HALLELUJAH.

1086. HOSANNA TO THE SON OF DAVID. I PRAISE YOU JESUS, HALLELUJAH.

1087. I THANK YOU FOR YOUR GUIDANCE, I WORSHIP YOU JESUS, HALLELUJAH.

1088. I THANK YOU FOR PROTECTION, I WORSHIP YOU JESUS, HALLELUJAH.

1089. I THANK YOU FOR YOUR KINGDOM, I WORSHIP YOU JESUS, HALLELUJAH.

1090. I THANK YOU FOR OUR RELATIONSHIP, I WORSHIP YOU JESUS, HALLELUJAH.

1091. I THANK YOU FOR MY HAPPINESS, I WORSHIP YOU JESUS, HALLELUJAH.
1092. I THANK YOU FOR YOUR GLORY, I WORSHIP YOU JESUS, HALLELUJAH.
1093. I THANK YOU FOR MY PRIESTHOOD, I WORSHIP YOU JESUS, HALLELUJAH.
1094. I THANK YOU FOR MY ANNOINTING, I WORSHIP YOU JESUS, HALLELUJAH.
1095. I THANK YOU FOR YOUR MERCY, I WORSHIP YOU JESUS, HALLELUJAH.
1096. I THANK YOU FOR MY SALVATION, I WORSHIP YOU JESUS, HALLELUJAH.
1097. I THANK YOU FOR MY KNOWLEDGE, I WORSHIP YOU JESUS, HALLELUJAH.
1098. I THANK YOU FOR MY UNDERSTANDING, I WORSHIP YOU JESUS, HALLELUJAH.
1099. I THANK YOU FOR REMOVING ALL CURSES FROM MY LIFE, I WORSHIP YOU JESUS, HALLELUJAH.
1100. I THANK YOU FOR ASSIGNING ANGELS TO ME, I WORSHIP YOU JESUS, HALLELUJAH.
1101. I THANK YOU FOR GIVING ME A SPIRITUAL TONGUE, I WORSHIP YOU JESUS, HALLELUJAH.
1102. I THANK YOU FOR ALL YOUR GIFTS, I WORSHIP YOU JESUS, HALLELUJAH.
1103. I THANK YOU FOR YOUR HOLINESS, I WORSHIP YOU JESUS, HALLELUJAH.
1104. I THANK YOU FOR THE MUSIC OF THE WORLD, I WORSHIP YOU JESUS, HALLELUJAH.
1105. I THANK YOU FOR THE PEACE IN THE WORLD, I WORSHIP YOU JESUS, HALLELUJAH.
1106. I THANK YOU FOR THE PROTECTION OF ISRAEL, I WORSHIP YOU JESUS, HALLELUJAH.
1107. I THANK YOU FOR THE PROTECTION OF THE POOR, I WORSHIP YOU JESUS, HALLELUJAH.
1108. I THANK YOU FOR LIFE, I WORSHIP YOU JESUS, HALLELUJAH.

1109. I THANK YOU FOR ETERNAL LIFE, I WORSHIP YOU JESUS, HALLELUJAH.

1110. I THANK YOU FOR THE HOLY SPIRIT, I WORSHIP YOU JESUS, HALLELUJAH.

1111. I THANK YOU FOR ACCEPTING MY UNDEFILED OFFERINGS, I WORSHIP YOU JESUS, HALLELUJAH.

1112. I THANK YOU FOR SHEDDING YOUR BLOOD FOR ME, I WORSHIP YOU JESUS, HALLELUJAH.

1113. I THANK YOU FOR YOUR EXALTATION, I WORSHIP YOU JESUS, HALLELUJAH.

1114. I THANK YOU FOR GIVING ME ACCESS TO HEAVEN, I WORSHIP YOU JESUS, HALLELUJAH.

1115. I THANK YOU FOR OVERCOMING ALL DISEASES, I WORSHIP YOU JESUS, HALLELUJAH.

1116. I THANK YOU FOR YOUR MIRACLES, I WORSHIP YOU JESUS, HALLELUJAH.

1117. I THANK YOU FOR PROTECTING THE WIDOW, I WORSHIP YOU JESUS, HALLELUJAH.

1118. I THANK YOU FOR PROTECTING THE CHILDREN, I WORSHIP YOU JESUS, HALLELUJAH.

1119. I KNOW YOU LIVE TODAY LORD, I WORSHIP YOU JESUS, HALLELUJAH.

1120. I KNOW YOU ARE WAITING FOR ME TO SEEK YOU LORD, I WORSHIP YOU JESUS, HALLELUJAH.

1121. I KNOW YOU WANT TO SHOW YOURSELF TO ME LORD, I WORSHIP YOU JESUS, HALLELUJAH.

1122. YOU ARE THE ALPHA AND OMEGA LORD, I WORSHIP YOU JESUS, HALLELUJAH.

1123. NOTHING WAS MADE WITHOUT YOUR KNOWLEDGE LORD, I WORSHIP YOU JESUS, HALLELUJAH.

1124. YOU AND THE FATHER JEHOVAH ARE ONE LORD, I WORSHIP YOU JESUS, HALLELUJAH.

1125. YOU ARE THE KING OF KINGS AND THE LORD OF LORDS, I WORSHIP YOU JESUS, HALLELUJAH.

1126. YOU ARE HE WHO SITS ON THE THRONE, I WORSHIP YOU JESUS, HALLELUJAH.
1127. YOU ARE THE HOLY ONE OF ISRAEL, I WORSHIP YOU JESUS, HALLELUJAH.
1128. YOU ARE THE ONE THAT THE MAGI WORSHIPED, I PRAISE YOU JESUS, HALLELUJAH.
1129. YOU ARE THE BRIGHT MORNING STAR, I PRAISE YOU JESUS, HALLELUJAH.
1130. YOU ARE THE TRUE KING OF THE JEWS, I PRAISE YOU JESUS, HALLELUJAH.
1131. YOU ARE THE MESSIAH TO COME, I PRAISE YOU JESUS, HALLELUJAH.
1132. YOU ARE THE ONLY SON OF GOD, I PRAISE YOU JESUS, HALLELUJAH.
1133. YOU WERE BORN FROM THE VIRGIN MARY, I WORSHIP YOU JESUS, HALLELUJAH.
1134. YOUR NAME IS EMANUEL, GOD WITH ME, I PRAISE YOU JESUS, HALLELUJAH.
1135. I PRAISE YOU JESUS, WHO WAS BORN IN BETHLEHEM, HALLELUJAH.
1136. I PRAISE YOU JESUS, WHO WAS BAPTIZED BY JOHN THE BAPTIST, HALLELUJAH.
1137. I PRAISE YOU JESUS, WHO HAS THE FULL RIGHTEOUSNESS OF GOD, HALLELUJAH.
1138. I PRAISE YOU JESUS, WHO OVERCAME ALL TEMPTATIONS, HALLELUJAH.
1139.
1140. YOU ARE THE ONE WHO PREACHED REPENT FOR THE KINGDOM OF GOD IS NEAR, I PRAISE YOU JESUS, HALLELUJAH.
1141. YOU CHOSE THE TWELVE DISCIPLES, I PRAISE YOU JESUS HALLELUJAH.
1142. YES LORD, YOU THOUGHT YOUR DISCIPLES HOW TO BE FISHERS OF MEN, I PRAISE YOU JESUS HALLELUJAH.
1143. JESUS YOU HEALED ALL THE DISEASED AND SICK PEOPLE YOU FOUND, I PRAISE YOU JESUS.

1144. LORD YOU HELPED ALL THOSE WITH FAITH IN YOU, I PRAISE YOU JESUS.

1145. YOU HEALED EVERYONE THAT BELIEVED, I BELIEVE, I PRAISE YOU JESUS.

1146. I WILL WORK HARD FOR YOU LORD, I PRAISE YOU JESUS.

1147. LORD YOU CALM THE STORMS AND THE WINDS, I PRAISE YOU JESUS.

1148. LORD YOU DROVE OUT DEMONS, I PRAISE YOU JESUS.

1149. LORD YOU MADE THE BLIND SEE AND MUTE TALK, I PRAISE YOU JESUS.

1150. LORD YOU GAVE YOUR TWELVE DISCIPLES AUTHORITY TO DRIVE OUT EVIL SPIRITS AND TO HEAL EVERY DISEASE AND SICKNESS, I PRAISE YOU JESUS.

1151. LORD YOU SAID YOU WILL DELIVER ME AND THAT IS WHAT I BELIEVE, I PRAISE YOU JESUS.

1152. LORD YOU DID IT JUST FOR ME, I PRAISE YOU JESUS.

1153. JOHN THE BAPTIST TALKED ABOUT YOU LORD, I PRAISE YOU JESUS.

1154. ABRAHAM SAW YOU LORD AND HE WAS GLAD, I PRAISE YOU JESUS.

1155. WOE TO THOSE WHO DON'T REPENT BUT, I WILL LORD, I PRAISE YOU JESUS.

1156. I PRAISE YOU JESUS, FOR REVEALING THE WISE THINGS TO ME, HALLELUJAH.

1157. LORD I HONOR YOU AND I PRAISE YOU JESUS, HALLELUJAH.

1158. LORD TEACH ME TO WALK ON WATER, I PRAISE YOU JESUS.

1159. I PRAISE YOU JESUS FOR SHOWING HOW GREAT MIRACLES COULD BE DONE.

1160. I PRAISE YOU JESUS FOR BEING THE GOD OF ALL GODS.

1161. I PRAISE YOU JESUS FOR SUPPLYING MY EVERY NEED.

1162. I PRAISE YOU JESUS FOR BEING MY ADVOCATE.
1163. I PRAISE YOU JESUS FOR PRAYING FOR MY SALVATION.
1164. LORD YOU CARRY A NAME ABOVE ALL OTHER NAMES, I PRAISE YOU JESUS.
1165. HOSANNA IN THE HIGHEST! I PRAISE YOU JESUS, HALLELUJAH.
1166. HOSANNA IN THE HIGHEST! BLESSED IS HE WHO COMES IN THE NAME OF THE LORD! I PRAISE YOU JESUS, HALLELUJAH.
1167. HOSANNA TO THE SON OF DAVID. I PRAISE YOU JESUS, HALLELUJAH.
1168. HOLY HOLY HOLY IS THE LORD GOD ALMIGHTY JESUS CHRIST, I PRAISE YOU JESUS.
1169. HOLY HOLY HOLY IS THE LORD GOD ALMIGHTY JESUS CHRIST, I PRAISE YOU JESUS.
1170. HOLY HOLY HOLY IS THE LORD GOD ALMIGHTY JESUS CHRIST, I PRAISE YOU JESUS.
1171. HOLY HOLY HOLY IS THE LORD GOD ALMIGHTY JESUS CHRIST, I PRAISE YOU JESUS.
1172. HOLY HOLY HOLY IS THE LORD GOD ALMIGHTY JESUS CHRIST, I PRAISE YOU JESUS.
1173. HOLY HOLY HOLY IS THE LORD GOD ALMIGHTY JESUS CHRIST, I PRAISE YOU JESUS.
1174. HOLY HOLY HOLY IS THE LORD GOD ALMIGHTY JESUS CHRIST, I PRAISE YOU JESUS.
1175. HALLELUJAH, HALLELUJAH, HALLELUJAH, I PRAISE YOU JESUS.
1176. HALLELUJAH, HALLELUJAH, HALLELUJAH, I PRAISE YOU JESUS.
1177. HALLELUJAH, HALLELUJAH, HALLELUJAH, I PRAISE YOU JESUS.
1178. HALLELUJAH, HALLELUJAH, HALLELUJAH, I PRAISE YOU JESUS.
1179. HALLELUJAH, HALLELUJAH, HALLELUJAH, I PRAISE YOU JESUS.

1180. HALLELUJAH, HALLELUJAH, HALLELUJAH, I PRAISE YOU JESUS.

1181. HALLELUJAH, HALLELUJAH, HALLELUJAH, I PRAISE YOU JESUS.

1182. GREAT IS YOUR MERCY LORD, I PRAISE YOU JESUS.

1183. LORD YOU ARE THE ORIGINAL SON OF MAN, I PRAISE YOU JESUS.

1184. I LOVE YOU JESUS, I PRAISE YOU GOD, HALLELUJAH.

1185. ONLY YOU ARE HOLY, I PRAISE YOU JESUS.

1186. ONLY YOU ARE HOLY, I PRAISE YOU JESUS, HALLELUJAH.

1187. ONLY YOU ARE HOLY JESUS, HALLELUJAH.

1188. THE SPIRIT SEARCHES ALL THOUGHTS EVEN YOUR OWN THOUHTS JESUS, I PRAISE YOU GOD ALMIGHTY, HALLELUJAH.

1189. YOU PROVIDE YOUR MYSTERIES, THE HIDDEN WISDOM PREDESTINED BEFORE THE AGES TO MY GLORY, I THANK YOU JESUS, HALLELUJAH.

1190. JESUS YOU WERE PRESENT, WHEN THERE WERE NO DEPTHS, HALLELUJAH.

1191. JESUS YOU WERE PRESENT, WHEN THERE WERE NO SPRINGS ABOUNDING WITH WATER, HALLELUJAH.

1192. JESUS YOU WERE PRESENT, BEFORE THE MOUNTAINS WERE SETTLED, HALLELUJAH.

1193. JESUS YOU WERE PRESENT, BEFORE THE HILLS WERE BROUGHT FORTH, HALLELUJAH

1194. JESUS YOU WERE PRESENT, WHILE GOD THE FATHER HAD NOT YET MADE THE EARTH AND THE FIELDS, HALLELUJAH.

1195. JESUS YOU WERE PRESENT, BEFORE THE FIRST DUST OF THE WORLD, HALLELUJAH.

1196. JESUS YOU WERE PRESENT, WHEN GOD THE FATHER ESTABLISHED THE HEAVENS, HALLELUJAH.

1197. JESUS YOU WERE PRESENT, WHEN GOD THE FATHER INSCRIBED A CIRCLE ON THE FACE OF THE DEEP, HALLELUJAH.
1198. JESUS YOU WERE PRESENT, WHEN GOD THE FATHER MADE FIRM THE SKIES ABOVE, HALLELUJAH.
1199. JESUS YOU WERE PRESENT, WHEN THE SPRINGS OF THE DEEP BECAME FIXED, HALLELUJAH.
1200. JESUS YOU WERE PRESENT, WHEN GOD THE FATHER SET FORT THE SEA AND ITS BOUNDARY, HALLELUJAH.
1201. JESUS YOU WERE PRESENT, WHEN GOD THE FATHER MARKED OUT THE FOUNDATIONS OF THE EARTH, HALLELUJAH.
1202. JESUS YOU WERE PRESENT, BESIDE GOD THE FATHER, AS A MASTER WORKMAN AND YOU WERE HIS DAILY DELIGHT, HALLELUJAH.
1203. JESUS YOU WERE PRESENT, REJOICING ALWAYS BEFORE GOD THE FATHER, HALLELUJAH.
1204. JESUS YOU WERE PRESENT, REJOICING IN THE WORLD, HALLELUJAH.
1205. JESUS YOU DELIGHTED IN THE SONS OF MEN, HALLELUJAH.
1206. JESUS, YOU SAID, SONS OF MEN LISTEN TO ME, I WILL LISTEN TO YOU LORD, HALLELUJAH.
1207. JESUS, YOU SAID, BLESSED ARE THEY WHO KEEP MY WAYS, I WILL, I PRAISE YOU, HALLELUJAH.
1208. JESUS YOU WERE PRESENT, WHEN THE PIT AND SHEOL WERE CREATED, HALLELUJAH.
1209. GLORY TO JESUS THE KING, I PRAISE YOU LORD, HALLELUJAH.
1210. JESUS YOU ARE THE GREAT "I AM," HALLELUJAH.
1211. I BELIEVE YOU LOVE ME LORD JESUS, HALLELUJAH.
1212. I BELIEVE IN YOUR POWER AND TRUTH LORD JESUS, HALLELUJAH.

1213. I BELIEVE YOU CAN DO ALL THINGS LORD JESUS, I PRAISE YOU LORD.

1214. I BELIEVE IN THE GLORY OF GOD, I PRAISE YOU LORD JESUS, HALLELUJAH.

1215. I BELIEVE YOU CAN RAISE THE DEAD TODAY JUST LIKE YESTERDAY, I PRAISE YOU GOD JESUS.

1216. I BELIEVE YOU CAN MAKE THE BLIND SEE AND THE DEAF HEAR LORD JESUS, HALLELUJAH.

1217. I BELIEVE YOU CAN MAKE THE CRIPPLE WALK, I PRAISE YOU LORD JESUS.

1218. I BELIEVE YOU CAN MAKE THE MENTALLY ILL HEALTHY, I PRAISE YOU LORD JESUS.

1219. I BELIEVE YOU CAN MAKE THE DUMB TALK, I PRAISE YOU LORD JESUS.

1220. I BELIEVE YOU ARE PRESENT AT ALL TIMES LORD, I PRAISE YOU LORD JESUS.

1221. I BELIEVE IN YOUR HEALING POWER LORD JESUS, I PRAISE YOU.

1222. I PRAISE YOU FOR MAKING ME HEIRS WITH YOU LORD, HALLELUJAH JESUS.

1223. I BELONG TO GOD AND I AM GLAD, HALLELUJAH JESUS.

1224. JESUS YOU MAKE MY DAYS BRIGHT AND MY NIGHTS COMFORTING, HALLELUJAH.

1225. JESUS YOU GIVE MY LIFE MEANING, I PRAISE YOU LORD.

1226. WORTHY IS THE LAMB MY LORD AND GOD JESUS, HALLELUJAH.

1227. WORTHY IS THE LAMB, YOU ARE HOLY MY LORD AND GOD JESUS, HALLELUJAH.

1228. WORTHY IS THE LAMB, I PRAISE YOU LORD JESUS, HALLELUJAH.

1229. THERE IS NO ONE ELSE LIKE YOU, I PRAISE YOU LORD JESUS.

1230. MY LIFE IS A TESTAMONY TO YOU LORD JESUS CHRIST, HALLELUJAH.

1231. I TRUST YOU LORD JESUS, I PRAISE YOU, HALLELUJAH.

1232. YOU WALK IN AUTHORITY LORD JESUS, I PRAISE YOU, HALLELUJAH.

1233. I CLAP MY HANDS IN PRAISES TO YOU LORD JESUS, HALLELUJAH.

1234. THERE IS NO OTHER GOD BUT YOU GOD ALMIGHTY JEHOVAH, HALLELUJAH.

1235. I LOVE YOU JESUS WITH MY WHOLE HEART, I PRAISE YOU LORD.

1236. I LEEP FOR JOY WITH YOU IN MY HEART LORD JESUS, HALLELUJAH.

1237. I DANCE LIKE DAVID FOR YOU LORD JESUS, HALLELUJAH.

1238. YOU SAID YOU WILL DELIVER ME LORD JESUS AND, I BELIEVE YOU, HALLELUJAH.

1239. YOU INSPIRE ME LORD JESUS, I PRAISE YOU LORD.

1240. YOU ARE MY WISDOM LORD JESUS, I PRAISE YOU.

1241. YOU ARE MY CREATIVITY LORD JESUS, I PRAISE YOU.

1242. YOU ARE MY DREAMS LORD JESUS, I PRAISE YOU.

1243. YOU ARE MY DESIRES LORD JESUS, I PRAISE YOU.

1244. YOU ARE MY ASPIRATIONS LORD JESUS, I PRAISE YOU.

1245. YOU ARE MY GOALS LORD JESUS, I PRAISE YOU.

1246. JESUS YOU ARE THE BREAD OF ALL LIFE, HALLELUJAH.

1247. JESUS YOU WERE THE ROCK IN HOREB, HALLELUJAH.

1248. JESUS YOU WERE THE SPIRITUAL ROCK IN THE DESERT, HALLELUJAH.

1249. JESUS YOU WERE THE PERFECT ROCK IN THE DESERT, HALLELUJAH.

1250. JESUS YOU ARE THE JUST ROCK, HALLELUJAH.
1251. JESUS YOU ARE THE UPRIGHT ROCK, HALLELUJAH.
1252. JESUS YOU ARE THE RIGHTEOUS ROCK, HALLELUJAH.
1253. JESUS YOU ARE THE ROCK FULL OF HONEY, HALLELUJAH.
1254. JESUS YOU ARE THE OIL FROM THE FLINTY ROCK, HALLELUJAH.
1255. JESUS YOU ARE THE ROCK WHO GAVE BIRTH TO ALL MANKIND, HALLELUJAH.
1256. JESUS YOU ARE THE SACRIFICIAL ROCK, HALLELUJAH.
1257. THERE IS NO ROCK HOLIER THAN YOU LORD JESUS, HALLELUJAH.
1258. I HAVE NO OTHER GOD BUT YOU JESUS, HALLELUJAH.
1259. MY LORD JESUS CHRIST LIVES FOREVER, I PRAISE YOU, HALLELUJAH.
1260. MY LORD LIVES NOW, PRAISE BE TO MY ROCK, JESUS.
1261. YOU ARE MY ROCK AND MY FORTRESS LORD JESUS, HALLELUJAH.
1262. YOU ARE MY GUIDE JESUS, I PRAISE YOU LORD JESUS.
1263. IN MY GOD JESUS IS MY SALVATION AND GLORY, HALLELUJAH.
1264. JESUS YOU ARE THE ROCK OF MY STRENGTH, HALLELUJAH.
1265. MY REFUGE IS IN YOU MY LORD JESUS, HALLELUJAH.
1266. YOU ARE MY MOST HIGH GOD AND MY REDEEMER LORD JESUS, HALLELUJAH.
1267. YOUR GLORY AND MAJESTY WILL PROTECT ME FOREVER LORD JESUS, HALLELUJAH.
1268. THE WISE MEN BUILD THEIR HOUSES ON YOUR ROCK LORD JESUS, HALLELUJAH.

1269. THE COST OF MY SINS I WILL NEVER KNOW, I THANK YOU AND WORSHIP YOU LORD JESUS, HALLELUJAH.

1270. I GIVE YOU THE HIGHEST PRAISE LORD JESUS, HALLELUJAH.

1271. LORD JESUS, YOU HAVE SAVED MY SOUL, HALLELUJAH.

1272. POUR OUT YOUR SPIRIT ON ME LORD JESUS, HALLELUJAH.

1273. LORD JESUS WHEN I THINK OF YOU I DANCE WITH JOY, HALLELUJAH.

1274. JESUS YOU DIED, TO SAVE ME, I PRAISE YOU LORD JESUS, HALLELUJAH.

1275. JESUS YOU DIED, SO I AM HEALED, I PRAISE YOU LORD JESUS, HALLELUJAH.

1276. JESUS YOU DIED, SO I OBTAIN GLORY, I PRAISE YOU LORD JESUS, HALLELUJAH.

1277. JESUS YOU DIED, SO I OBTAIN LIFE, I PRAISE YOU LORD JESUS, HALLELUJAH.

1278. JESUS YOU DIED, TO MAKE ME HAPPY, I PRAISE YOU LORD JESUS, HALLELUJAH.

1279. JESUS YOU DIED, TO GIVE ME HOPE, I PRAISE YOU LORD JESUS, HALLELUJAH.

1280. JESUS YOU DIED, TO GIVE ME YOUR RIGHTEOUSNESS, I PRAISE YOU LORD JESUS, HALLELUJAH.

1281. JESUS YOU DIED, FOR US TO BE TOGETHER, I PRAISE YOU LORD JESUS, HALLELUJAH.

1282. JESUS YOU DIED, TO FREE ME FROM SIN, I PRAISE YOU LORD JESUS, HALLELUJAH.

1283. JESUS YOU DIED, TO GIVE ME ETERNAL LIFE, I PRAISE YOU LORD JESUS, HALLELUJAH.

1284. JESUS YOU DIED, FOR ME TO DEVELOP A RELATIONSHIP WITH YOU, I PRAISE YOU LORD JESUS, HALLELUJAH.

1285. JESUS YOU DIED, FOR ME TO DEVELOP A RELATIONSHIP WITH FATHER GOD, I PRAISE YOU LORD JESUS, HALLELUJAH.

1286. JESUS YOU DIED, FOR ME TO DEVELOP A RELATIONSHIP WITH THE HOLY SPIRIT, I PRAISE YOU LORD JESUS, HALLELUJAH.
1287. JESUS YOU DIED, TO SHOW ME ALL THE SECRETS OF HEAVEN, I PRAISE YOU LORD JESUS, HALLELUJAH.
1288. JESUS YOU DIED, FOR ME TO KNOW WHAT TRUE LOVE IS, I PRAISE YOU LORD JESUS, HALLELUJAH.
1289. JESUS YOU DIED, SO I KNOW WHAT TRUE OBEDIENCE IS, I PRAISE YOU LORD JESUS, HALLELUJAH.
1290. JESUS I AM YOUR AMBASSADOR FOR LIFE, I WILL WORSHIP YOU FOREVER, AMEN, I PRAISE YOU, HALLELUJAH
1291. YOU ARE MY COUNSELOR JESUS I PRAISE YOU LORD JESUS, HALLELUJAH.
1292. MY HELP COMES FROM THE LORD JESUS, THE MAKER OF HEAVEN AND EARTH, I WORSHIP YOU JESUS, HALLELUJAH.

MEDITATE AND ASK JEHOVAH TO OPEN YOUR EYES

1 CORINTHIANS 1:18-30

LISTEN PASTORS AND MEN OF JEHOVAH

THE MESSAGE OF THE CROSS IS FOOLISHNESS TO
THOSE WHO ARE PERISHING,

(THE MESSAGE OF THE CROSS IS THE POWER OF
GOD AND THE UNITY OF THE BODY)

FOR IT IS WRITTEN:
"I WILL DESTROY THE WISDOM OF THE WISE;

THE INTELLIGENCE OF THE INTELLIGENT I WILL
FRUSTRATE."

JEWS DEMAND MIRACULOUS SIGNS AND GENTILES
LOOK FOR WISDOM,

FOR THE FOOLISHNESS OF GOD IS WISER THAN
MAN'S WISDOM,

THE WEAKNESS OF GOD IS STRONGER THAN
MAN'S STRENGTH.

PASTORS, THINK OF WHAT YOU WERE WHEN
YOU WERE CALLED. NOT MANY OF YOU WERE
WISE BY HUMAN STANDARDS; NOT MANY WERE
INFLUENTIAL; NOT MANY WERE OF NOBLE BIRTH.
BUT GOD CHOSE THE FOOLISH THINGS OF THE
WORLD TO SHAME THE
WISE;

GOD CHOSE THE WEAK THINGS OF THE WORLD
TO SHAME THE STRONG.
HE CHOSE THE LOWLY THINGS OF THIS WORLD
AND THE DESPISED THINGS
—AND THE THINGS THAT ARE NOT—
TO NULLIFY THE THINGS THAT ARE,
SO THAT NO ONE MAY BOAST BEFORE HIM.

MEDITATE AND ASK JEHOVAH TO OPEN YOUR EYES

EVERY NATION WHO TRIES TO DESTROY ISRAEL WILL BE DESTROYED

ZEPHANIAH 2:8-11
AGAINST MOAB AND AMMON

"I HAVE HEARD THE INSULTS OF MOAB
AND THE TAUNTS OF THE AMMONITES,
WHO INSULTED MY PEOPLE
AND MADE THREATS AGAINST THEIR LAND.

THEREFORE,
AS SURELY AS I LIVE,"

DECLARES THE LORD ALMIGHTY, THE GOD OF
ISRAEL,

"SURELY MOAB WILL BECOME LIKE SODOM,
THE AMMONITES LIKE GOMORRAH—
A PLACE OF WEEDS AND SALT PITS,
A WASTELAND FOREVER.

THE REMNANT OF MY PEOPLE WILL PLUNDER
THEM;
THE SURVIVORS OF MY NATION WILL INHERIT
THEIR LAND."
THIS IS WHAT THEY WILL GET IN RETURN FOR
THEIR PRIDE,
FOR INSULTING AND MOCKING THE PEOPLE OF
THE LORD ALMIGHTY.

THE LORD WILL BE AWESOME TO THEM
WHEN HE DESTROYS ALL THE GODS OF THE LAND.

THE NATIONS ON EVERY SHORE WILL WORSHIP
HIM

THE WHOLE WORLD WILL WORSHIP THE GOD OF
ISRAEL,

EVERYONE IN ITS OWN LAND.

MEDITATE AND ASK JEHOVAH TO OPEN YOUR EYES

JESUS PRAYS FOR UNITY OF THE CHURCH

EVERYTHING JESUS PRAYS FOR WILL HAPPEN, BECAUSE HE SAID SO.

JOHN 11:42

42 I KNEW THAT YOU ALWAYS HEAR ME,
BUT I SAID THIS FOR THE BENEFIT OF THE PEOPLE
STANDING HERE,
THAT THEY MAY BELIEVE THAT YOU SENT ME."
JOHN 17:20-23
JESUS PRAYS FOR ALL BELIEVERS

"MY PRAYER IS NOT FOR THEM ALONE.

I PRAY ALSO FOR THOSE WHO WILL BELIEVE IN ME
THROUGH THEIR MESSAGE,

THAT ALL OF THEM MAY BE ONE, FATHER, JUST AS
YOU ARE IN ME AND I AM IN YOU.

MAY THEY ALSO BE IN US SO THAT THE WORLD
MAY BELIEVE THAT YOU HAVE SENT ME.

I HAVE GIVEN THEM THE GLORY THAT YOU GAVE
ME, THAT THEY MAY BE ONE AS WE ARE ONE:

I IN THEM AND YOU IN ME.

MAY THEY BE BROUGHT TO COMPLETE UNITY

TO LET THE WORLD KNOW THAT YOU SENT ME

AND

HAVE LOVED THEM EVEN AS YOU HAVE LOVED ME.
MATTHEW 28:18
18 THEN JESUS CAME TO THEM AND SAID,
"ALL AUTHORITY IN HEAVEN AND ON EARTH HAS
BEEN GIVEN TO ME.

MEDITATE AND ASK JEHOVAH TO OPEN YOUR EYES

WE ALL ARE TO BE TAUGHT UNITY, BY THE CHURCH.

EPHESIANS 4:10-15

NEW INTERNATIONAL VERSION 1984 (NIV1984)

10 HE WHO DESCENDED IS THE VERY ONE WHO ASCENDED
HIGHER THAN ALL THE HEAVENS,
IN ORDER TO FILL THE WHOLE UNIVERSE.

11 IT WAS HE WHO GAVE SOME TO BE APOSTLES,
SOME TO BE PROPHETS, SOME TO BE EVANGELISTS,
AND SOME TO BE PASTORS AND TEACHERS,

12 TO PREPARE GOD'S PEOPLE FOR WORKS OF SERVICE,
SO THAT THE BODY OF CHRIST MAY BE BUILT UP

13 UNTIL WE ALL REACH UNITY IN THE FAITH
AND IN THE KNOWLEDGE OF THE SON OF GOD
AND BECOME MATURE,
ATTAINING TO THE WHOLE MEASURE OF THE
FULLNESS OF CHRIST.

14 THEN WE WILL NO LONGER BE INFANTS,
TOSSED BACK AND FORTH BY THE WAVES,
AND BLOWN HERE AND THERE BY EVERY WIND OF TEACHING

AND BY THE CUNNING AND CRAFTINESS OF MEN
IN THEIR DECEITFUL SCHEMING.

15 INSTEAD, SPEAKING THE TRUTH IN LOVE,
WE WILL IN ALL THINGS GROW UP INTO HIM
WHO IS THE HEAD,

THAT IS, CHRIST.

MEDITATE AND ASK JEHOVAH TO OPEN YOUR EYES

UNITY AND DIVERSITY IN THE BODY

1 CORINTHIANS 12:12-31

JUST AS A BODY,
THOUGH ONE,
HAS MANY PARTS,
BUT
ALL ITS MANY PARTS FORM ONE BODY,
SO IT IS WITH CHRIST.

ROMANS 12:5
SO IN CHRIST WE,
THOUGH MANY,
FORM ONE BODY,
AND
EACH MEMBER BELONGS TO ALL THE OTHERS
ALL CHRISTIAN ORGANIZATIONS WORLD WIDE
INCLUDING THE JEWS
OR
ALL THE ELECT WORLD WIDE IS ONE BODY
ROMANS 11:25
I DO NOT WANT YOU TO BE IGNORANT OF THIS
MYSTERY, BROTHERS, SO THAT YOU MAY NOT BE
CONCEITED:
ISRAEL HAS EXPERIENCED A HARDENING IN PART
UNTIL;
THE FULL NUMBER OF THE GENTILES HAS COME
IN.
WE SHALL BUILD BLOCK BY BLOCK
BEFORE JESUS COMES AGAIN: WE HAVE THE TOOLS

MEDITATE AND ASK JEHOVAH TO OPEN YOUR EYES

UNITY IN THE BODY OF JESUS CHRIST IS NEEDED

1 CORINTHIANS 10

I APPEAL TO YOU, BROTHERS

(ALL OF GOD'S ELECT, JEWS AND GENTILES),

IN THE NAME OF OUR LORD JESUS CHRIST,

THAT ALL OF YOU AGREE WITH ONE ANOTHER

SO THAT THERE MAY BE NO DIVISIONS AMONG YOU

AND THAT YOU MAY BE PERFECTLY UNITED

IN MIND AND THOUGHT.

IS PAUL ONLY SPEAKING TO ONE CHURCH OR ALL CHURCHES?

IF THE CHURCHES CLAIM THEY LOVE CHRIST AND WE ALL HAVE THE ONE SPIRIT OF JESUS CHRIST THEN,
WHAT IS THE PROBLEM IN PUTTING TOGETHER A UNIFIED CHURCH?

MEDITATE AND ASK JEHOVAH TO OPEN YOUR EYES

UNITY IN THE BODY OF JESUS CHRIST WORLD WIDE IS NEEDED

THE ELECT JEWS AND GENTILES HAVE ONE SPIRIT THAT GOVERNS ALL

1 CORINTHIANS 12:13

FOR WE WERE ALL BAPTIZED BY ONE SPIRIT

INTO ONE BODY

—WHETHER JEWS OR GENTILES, SLAVE OR FREE—

AND WE WERE ALL

GIVEN THE ONE SPIRIT TO DRINK.

MEDITATE AND ASK JEHOVAH TO OPEN YOUR EYES

JEWS AND GENTILES ELECT ARE ONE BODY

WE CANNOT CONVINCE PEOPLE WITHOUT CHRIST BEING IN US.

JOHN 15:4
JESUS SAID,

(SPEAKING TO HIS JEWISH BELIEVERS)
"ABIDE IN ME, AND I IN YOU.
AS THE BRANCH CANNOT BEAR FRUIT OF ITSELF,
UNLESS IT ABIDES IN THE VINE,
NEITHER CAN YOU,
UNLESS YOU ABIDE IN ME."

JOHN 15:5

"I AM THE VINE,

YOU ARE THE BRANCHES.

HE WHO ABIDES IN ME,

AND I IN HIM,

BEARS MUCH FRUIT;

FOR WITHOUT ME YOU CAN DO NOTHING.

MEDITATE AND ASK JEHOVAH TO OPEN YOUR EYES

THE JEWS NEED TO WAKE UP

JEHOVAH HATES PRIDE

TODAY WE HAVE JEWS WHO CLAIM TO BELIEVE IN JESUS AS THE MESSIAH BUT, THEY DON'T WANT TO BE CALLED CHRISTIANS. THEY WANT TO BE CALLED MESSIANIC JEWS. THIS IS PRIDE. (SEE BELOW) JESUS HAS ONE BODY, NOT TWO. SATAN CONTINUES TO CONFUSE THE JEWS ABOUT THEIR OWN GOD, JEHOVAH AND THEIR OWN MESSIAH, OUR LORD AND SAVIOR JESUS CHRIST. THE JEWS SOLD THE WORLD ON BUYING INTO THEIR GOD, JEHOVAH. NOW, THEY ARE PLAYING SIMANTICS TO SEPARATE THE WORLD FROM THEM. JEWS, LISTEN TO ME, YOU CANNOT FIGHT THE WORLD ON YOUR OWN. JESUS HAS RECRUITED PEOPLE TO LOVE YOU AND HELP YOU. JESUS TOLD US TO LOVE GOD WITH ALL OUR HEARTS AND TO LOVE OUR NEIGHBORS. YOU ARE EVEN MORE THAN A NEIGHBOR TO THE GENTILE ELECT.

I DON'T UNDERSTAND THE JEWS POINT BECAUSE CHRISTIANITY WAS STARTED BY JEWS. GENTILES DID NOT CREATE CHRISTIANITY. GENTILES ACTUALLY BELIEVED EVERYTHING THEY WERE TAUGHT BY THE JEWS ABOUT JESUS. THE JEWS DOCUMENTED AND HAD GREAT PROOF TO SHOW THAT JESUS WAS THE MESSIAH, THEY WERE WAITING FOR. THE TERM CHRISTIANITY ACTUALLY IS THE TYPE OF MESSAGE JESUS WANTED TO SEND, AND THE TERM WAS NOT CREATED BY GENTILES. JESUS SAID HE BROUGHT

A NEW COVERNANT WITH SOME OF THE OLD CHARACTERISTICS. HENCE, BECAUSE THERE WAS GOING TO BE A CHANGE IN THE OLD COVERNANT, THE NAME HAD TO ALSO CHANGE. JESUS EXPLAINED IT THE FOLLOWING WAY;

LUKE 5:36-39

HE TOLD THEM THIS PARABLE: "NO ONE TEARS A PATCH FROM A NEW GARMENT AND SEWS IT ON AN OLD ONE. IF HE DOES, HE WILL HAVE TORN THE NEW GARMENT, AND THE PATCH FROM THE NEW WILL NOT MATCH THE OLD. 37 AND NO ONE POURS NEW WINE INTO OLD WINESKINS. IF HE DOES, THE NEW WINE WILL BURST THE SKINS, THE WINE WILL RUN OUT AND THE WINESKINS WILL BE RUINED. 38 NO, NEW WINE MUST BE POURED INTO NEW WINESKINS. 39 AND NO ONE AFTER DRINKING OLD WINE WANTS THE NEW, FOR HE SAYS, 'THE OLD IS BETTER.'"

JEHOVAH HATES PRIDE

1.   PROVERBS 8:13
TO FEAR THE LORD IS TO HATE EVIL; I HATE PRIDE
AND ARROGANCE, EVIL BEHAVIOR AND PERVERSE
SPEECH.

2.   PROVERBS 11:2
WHEN PRIDE COMES, THEN COMES DISGRACE,
BUT WITH HUMILITY COMES WISDOM.

3.   PROVERBS 13:10
PRIDE ONLY BREEDS QUARRELS, BUT WISDOM IS
FOUND IN THOSE WHO TAKE ADVICE.

4.   PROVERBS 16:18
PRIDE GOES BEFORE DESTRUCTION, A HAUGHTY
SPIRIT BEFORE A FALL.

MEDITATE AND ASK JEHOVAH TO OPEN YOUR EYES

JEWS AND GENTILES ELECT ARE ONE BODY

WHAT EXPLANATION COULD YOUR CHURCH GIVE
FOR NOT WANTING TO UNITE
THE FULL BODY OF JESUS CHRIST?

EPHESIANS 3:6

THIS MYSTERY IS THAT THROUGH THE GOSPEL
THE

GENTILES ARE HEIRS TOGETHER WITH ISRAEL,
MEMBERS

TOGETHER OF ONE BODY, AND SHARERS
TOGETHER IN

THE PROMISE IN CHRIST JESUS.

EPHESIANS 1:22-23

AND GOD PLACED ALL THINGS UNDER HIS FEET AND

APPOINTED HIM TO BE HEAD OVER EVERYTHING
FOR THE

CHURCH, WHICH IS HIS BODY, THE FULLNESS OF
HIM WHO

FILLS EVERYTHING IN EVERY WAY.

MEDITATE AND ASK JEHOVAH TO OPEN YOUR EYES

ONE NEW MAN

EPHESIANS 2:1-22

AS FOR YOU(JEWS AND GENTILES), YOU WERE DEAD IN YOUR TRANSGRESSIONS AND SINS, IN WHICH YOU USED TO LIVE WHEN YOU FOLLOWED THE WAYS OF THIS WORLD AND OF THE RULER OF THE KINGDOM OF THE AIR(SATAN), THE SPIRIT WHO IS NOW AT WORK IN THOSE WHO ARE DISOBEDIENT. ALL OF US ALSO LIVED AMONG THEM AT ONE TIME, GRATIFYING THE CRAVINGS OF OUR SINFUL NATURE AND FOLLOWING ITS DESIRES AND THOUGHTS. LIKE THE REST(SINNERS), WE WERE BY NATURE OBJECTS OF WRATH. BUT BECAUSE OF HIS GREAT LOVE FOR US, GOD, WHO IS RICH IN MERCY, MADE US ALIVE WITH CHRIST EVEN WHEN WE WERE DEAD IN TRANSGRESSIONS—IT IS BY GRACE WE HAVE BEEN SAVED.
AND GOD RAISED US UP WITH CHRIST AND SEATED US WITH HIM IN THE HEAVENLY REALMS IN CHRIST JESUS,
IN ORDER THAT IN THE COMING AGES HE MIGHT SHOW THE INCOMPARABLE RICHES OF HIS GRACE, EXPRESSED IN HIS KINDNESS TO US IN CHRIST JESUS. FOR IT IS BY GRACE YOU HAVE BEEN SAVED, THROUGH FAITH—AND THIS NOT FROM YOURSELVES, IT IS THE GIFT OF GOD— NOT BY WORKS, SO THAT NO ONE CAN BOAST. FOR WE ARE GOD'S WORKMANSHIP, CREATED IN CHRIST JESUS TO DO GOOD WORKS, WHICH GOD PREPARED IN ADVANCE FOR US TO DO(ELIJAH).

THEREFORE, REMEMBER THAT FORMERLY YOU WHO ARE GENTILES BY BIRTH AND CALLED "UNCIRCUMCISED" BY THOSE WHO CALL THEMSELVES "THE CIRCUMCISION" (THAT DONE IN THE BODY BY THE HANDS OF MEN)— REMEMBER THAT AT THAT TIME YOU WERE SEPARATE FROM CHRIST, EXCLUDED FROM CITIZENSHIP IN ISRAEL AND FOREIGNERS TO THE COVENANTS OF THE PROMISE, WITHOUT HOPE AND WITHOUT GOD IN THE WORLD. BUT NOW IN CHRIST JESUS YOU WHO ONCE WERE FAR AWAY HAVE BEEN BROUGHT NEAR THROUGH THE BLOOD OF CHRIST.

FOR HE HIMSELF IS OUR PEACE, (WHO HAS MADE THE TWO ONE AND HAS DESTROYED THE BARRIER,) THE DIVIDING WALL OF HOSTILITY, BY ABOLISHING IN HIS FLESH THE LAW WITH ITS COMMANDMENTS AND REGULATIONS.

HIS PURPOSE WAS TO CREATE IN HIMSELF ONE NEW MAN(STICKS: EZEKIEL 37) OUT OF THE TWO, THUS MAKING PEACE, AND IN THIS ONE BODY TO RECONCILE BOTH OF THEM TO GOD THROUGH THE CROSS,

BY WHICH HE PUT TO DEATH THEIR HOSTILITY. HE CAME AND PREACHED PEACE TO YOU WHO WERE FAR AWAY(GENTILE)

AND PEACE TO THOSE WHO WERE NEAR(JEWS). FOR THROUGH HIM WE BOTH HAVE ACCESS TO THE FATHER BY ONE SPIRIT:(THE HOLY SPIRIT). CONSEQUENTLY, YOU ARE NO LONGER FOREIGNERS AND ALIENS, BUT FELLOW CITIZENS WITH GOD'S PEOPLE AND MEMBERS OF GOD'S HOUSEHOLD, BUILT ON THE FOUNDATION OF THE APOSTLES AND PROPHETS,

WITH CHRIST JESUS HIMSELF AS THE CHIEF CORNERSTONE. IN HIM THE WHOLE BUILDING IS JOINED TOGETHER

AND RISES TO BECOME A HOLY TEMPLE IN THE LORD. AND IN HIM YOU TOO(JEWS AND GENTILES) ARE BEING BUILT TOGETHER(JEWS AND GENTILES) TO BECOME A DWELLING IN WHICH GOD LIVES BY HIS SPIRIT(ONE NEW MAN GOVERN BY THE HOLY SPIRIT).

MEDITATE AND ASK JEHOVAH TO OPEN YOUR EYES

JEHOVAH WANTS ONE CHRISTIAN BODY IN HIS HAND.

UNITY IN THE CHURCH IS A PRIORITY FOR JESUS READ ON AND EXAMINE FOR YOURSELF WHAT JEHOVAH'S DESIRE IS.

EZEKIEL 37:15-28

ONE NATION UNDER ONE KING

THE WORD OF THE LORD CAME TO ME: "SON OF MAN, TAKE A STICK OF WOOD AND WRITE ON IT, 'BELONGING TO JUDAH(ALL CHRISTIANS ALSO PART OF JUDAH) AND THE ISRAELITES ASSOCIATED WITH HIM.' THEN TAKE ANOTHER STICK OF WOOD, AND WRITE ON IT, 'EPHRAIM'S STICK, BELONGING TO JOSEPH AND ALL THE HOUSE OF ISRAEL ASSOCIATED WITH HIM.' JOIN THEM TOGETHER INTO ONE STICK SO THAT THEY WILL BECOME ONE IN YOUR HAND(JEHOVAH WANTS UNITY, HE WANTS ONE BODY).
"WHEN YOUR COUNTRYMEN ASK YOU, 'WON'T YOU TELL US WHAT YOU MEAN BY THIS?' 19 SAY TO THEM, 'THIS IS WHAT THE SOVEREIGN LORD SAYS: I AM GOING TO TAKE THE STICK OF JOSEPH—WHICH IS IN EPHRAIM'S HAND—AND OF THE ISRAELITE TRIBES ASSOCIATED WITH HIM, AND JOIN IT TO JUDAH'S STICK, MAKING THEM A SINGLE STICK(ONE BODY) OF WOOD, AND THEY WILL BECOME ONE IN MY HAND.'

HOLD BEFORE THEIR EYES THE STICKS YOU HAVE WRITTEN ON AND SAY TO THEM,
'THIS IS WHAT THE SOVEREIGN LORD SAYS: I WILL TAKE THE ISRAELITES OUT OF THE NATIONS WHERE THEY HAVE GONE. I WILL GATHER THEM FROM ALL AROUND AND BRING THEM BACK INTO THEIR OWN LAND. I WILL MAKE THEM ONE NATION IN THE LAND, ON THE MOUNTAINS OF ISRAEL. THERE WILL BE ONE KING(JESUS CHRIST) OVER ALL OF THEM AND THEY WILL NEVER AGAIN BE TWO NATIONS OR BE DIVIDED INTO TWO KINGDOMS. THEY WILL NO LONGER DEFILE THEMSELVES WITH THEIR IDOLS AND VILE IMAGES OR WITH ANY OF THEIR OFFENSES, FOR I WILL SAVE THEM FROM ALL THEIR SINFUL BACKSLIDING, AND I WILL CLEANSE THEM. THEY WILL BE MY PEOPLE, AND I WILL BE THEIR GOD.

(ISRAEL WILL NOT BE DESTROYED OR MOVED)

"MY SERVANT DAVID(JESUS CHRIST) WILL BE KING OVER THEM, AND THEY WILL ALL HAVE ONE SHEPHERD. THEY WILL FOLLOW MY LAWS AND BE CAREFUL TO KEEP MY DECREES. THEY WILL LIVE IN THE LAND I GAVE TO MY SERVANT JACOB, THE LAND WHERE YOUR FATHERS LIVED. THEY AND THEIR CHILDREN AND THEIR CHILDREN'S CHILDREN WILL LIVE THERE FOREVER, AND DAVID MY SERVANT WILL BE THEIR PRINCE FOREVER. I WILL MAKE A COVENANT OF PEACE WITH THEM; IT WILL BE AN EVERLASTING COVENANT. I WILL ESTABLISH THEM AND INCREASE THEIR NUMBERS, AND I WILL PUT MY SANCTUARY AMONG THEM FOREVER. MY DWELLING PLACE WILL BE WITH THEM; I WILL BE THEIR GOD, AND THEY WILL BE MY PEOPLE. THEN THE NATIONS WILL KNOW THAT

I THE LORD MAKE ISRAEL HOLY(JESUS WILL MAKE ISRAEL HOLY. JESUS HAS THE AUTHORITY OVER HEAVEN AND EARTH.), WHEN MY SANCTUARY IS AMONG THEM FOREVER.'"

MEDITATE AND ASK JEHOVAH TO OPEN YOUR EYES

JESUS INTENTION IS ALWAYS TO BRING ALL

HIS PEOPLE INTO ONE BODY.

MATTHEW 23:37-39

"O JERUSALEM, JERUSALEM,

YOU WHO KILL THE PROPHETS AND STONE THOSE

SENT TO YOU,

HOW OFTEN I HAVE LONGED TO GATHER YOUR
CHILDREN TOGETHER,

AS A HEN GATHERS HER CHICKS UNDER HER
WINGS,

BUT YOU WERE NOT WILLING.

(PASTORS AND RABBIS TODAY ARE STILL NOT
WILLING)

LOOK, YOUR HOUSE IS LEFT TO YOU DESOLATE.

FOR

I TELL YOU, YOU WILL

NOT SEE ME AGAIN UNTIL

YOU SAY,

(THE JEWS SAY JESUS IS THE MESSIAH)

'BLESSED IS HE WHO

COMES IN THE NAME OF THE LORD.'"

MEDITATE AND ASK JEHOVAH TO OPEN YOUR EYES

THE ELECT MUST COME TOGETHER BEFORE JESUS RETURNS

WE ALL MUST ACCEPT JESUS AS THE MESSIAH

JEWS AND GENTILES

OR

WE WILL SUFFER WHEN HE RETURNS
ZEPHANIAH 2:1-3

GATHER TOGETHER, GATHER TOGETHER,

O SHAMEFUL NATION,

BEFORE THE APPOINTED TIME ARRIVES

AND THAT DAY SWEEPS ON LIKE CHAFF,

BEFORE THE FIERCE ANGER OF THE LORD COMES
UPON YOU,

BEFORE THE DAY OF THE LORD'S WRATH COMES
UPON YOU.

SEEK THE LORD, ALL YOU HUMBLE OF THE LAND,

YOU WHO DO WHAT HE COMMANDS.

SEEK RIGHTEOUSNESS(SEEK JESUS), SEEK HUMILITY;

PERHAPS YOU WILL BE SHELTERED

ON THE DAY OF THE LORD'S ANGER.
MEDITATE AND ASK JEHOVAH TO OPEN YOUR EYES

MATTHEW 23:1-28

SEVEN WOES

(PASTORS AND RABBIS TODAY)
ד,ח,א ה,וה,י וני,ה'ל,א ה,וה,י ל,א,ר, שי ע,מ, ש.

JESUS SAID TO THE CROWDS AND TO HIS DISCIPLES: "THE TEACHERS OF THE LAW AND THE PHARISEES(PASTORS AND RABBIS) SIT IN MOSES' SEAT. SO YOU MUST OBEY THEM AND DO EVERYTHING THEY TELL YOU. BUT DO NOT DO WHAT THEY DO, FOR THEY DO NOT PRACTICE WHAT THEY PREACH. THEY TIE UP HEAVY LOADS AND PUT THEM ON MEN'S SHOULDERS, BUT THEY THEMSELVES ARE NOT WILLING TO LIFT A FINGER TO MOVE THEM.

"EVERYTHING THEY DO IS DONE FOR MEN TO SEE: THEY MAKE THEIR PHYLACTERIES WIDE AND THE TASSELS ON THEIR GARMENTS LONG; THEY LOVE THE PLACE OF HONOR AT BANQUETS AND THE MOST IMPORTANT SEATS IN THE SYNAGOGUES; THEY LOVE TO BE GREETED IN THE MARKETPLACES AND TO HAVE MEN CALL THEM 'RABBI.'
"BUT YOU ARE NOT TO BE CALLED 'RABBI,' FOR YOU HAVE ONLY ONE MASTER AND YOU ARE ALL BROTHERS. AND DO NOT CALL ANYONE ON EARTH 'FATHER,' FOR YOU HAVE ONE FATHER, AND HE IS IN HEAVEN. NOR ARE YOU TO BE CALLED 'TEACHER,' FOR YOU HAVE ONE TEACHER, THE CHRIST. THE GREATEST AMONG YOU WILL BE YOUR SERVANT. FOR WHOEVER EXALTS HIMSELF WILL BE HUMBLED, AND WHOEVER HUMBLES HIMSELF WILL BE EXALTED.

"WOE TO YOU, TEACHERS OF THE LAW AND PHARISEES(PASTORS AND RABBIS), YOU HYPOCRITES! YOU SHUT THE KINGDOM OF HEAVEN IN MEN'S FACES. YOU YOURSELVES DO NOT ENTER, NOR WILL YOU LET THOSE ENTER WHO ARE TRYING TO.

"WOE TO YOU, TEACHERS OF THE LAW AND PHARISEES(PASTORS AND RABBIS), YOU HYPOCRITES! YOU TRAVEL OVER LAND AND SEA TO WIN A SINGLE CONVERT, AND WHEN HE BECOMES ONE, YOU MAKE HIM TWICE AS MUCH A SON OF HELL AS YOU ARE.

"WOE TO YOU, BLIND GUIDES! YOU SAY, 'IF ANYONE SWEARS BY THE TEMPLE, IT MEANS NOTHING; BUT IF ANYONE SWEARS BY THE GOLD OF THE TEMPLE, HE IS BOUND BY HIS OATH.' YOU BLIND FOOLS! WHICH IS GREATER: THE GOLD, OR THE TEMPLE THAT MAKES THE GOLD SACRED? YOU ALSO SAY, 'IF ANYONE SWEARS BY THE ALTAR, IT MEANS NOTHING; BUT IF ANYONE SWEARS BY THE GIFT ON IT, HE IS BOUND BY HIS OATH.' YOU BLIND MEN! WHICH IS GREATER: THE GIFT, OR THE ALTAR THAT MAKES THE GIFT SACRED? THEREFORE, HE WHO SWEARS BY THE ALTAR SWEARS BY IT AND BY EVERYTHING ON IT. AND HE WHO SWEARS BY THE TEMPLE SWEARS BY IT AND BY THE ONE WHO DWELLS IN IT. AND HE WHO SWEARS BY HEAVEN SWEARS BY GOD'S THRONE AND BY THE ONE WHO SITS ON IT.

"WOE TO YOU, TEACHERS OF THE LAW AND PHARISEES, YOU HYPOCRITES! YOU GIVE A TENTH OF YOUR SPICES—MINT, DILL AND CUMMIN. BUT YOU HAVE NEGLECTED THE MORE IMPORTANT MATTERS OF THE LAW—JUSTICE, MERCY AND FAITHFULNESS. YOU SHOULD HAVE PRACTICED THE LATTER, WITHOUT NEGLECTING THE FORMER. YOU BLIND GUIDES! YOU STRAIN OUT A GNAT BUT SWALLOW A CAMEL.

"WOE TO YOU, TEACHERS OF THE LAW AND PHARISEES(PASTORS AND RABBIS), YOU HYPOCRITES! YOU CLEAN THE OUTSIDE OF THE CUP AND

DISH, BUT INSIDE THEY ARE FULL OF GREED AND SELF-INDULGENCE. BLIND PHARISEE(PASTORS AND RABBIS)! FIRST CLEAN THE INSIDE OF THE CUP AND DISH, AND THEN THE OUTSIDE ALSO WILL BE CLEAN.

"WOE TO YOU, TEACHERS OF THE LAW AND PHARISEES(PASTORS AND RABBIS), YOU HYPOCRITES! YOU ARE LIKE WHITEWASHED TOMBS, WHICH LOOK BEAUTIFUL ON THE OUTSIDE BUT ON THE INSIDE ARE FULL OF DEAD MEN'S BONES AND EVERYTHING UNCLEAN. IN THE SAME WAY, ON THE OUTSIDE YOU APPEAR TO PEOPLE AS RIGHTEOUS BUT ON THE INSIDE YOU ARE FULL OF HYPOCRISY AND WICKEDNESS.

MEDITATE AND ASK JEHOVAH TO OPEN YOUR EYES

PAUL'S LETER TO THE JEWS OR GENTILES WHO WANT TO BE SAVED

ROMANS 10:1-21

BROTHERS, MY HEART'S DESIRE AND PRAYER TO GOD FOR THE ISRAELITES IS THAT THEY MAY BE SAVED. FOR I CAN TESTIFY ABOUT THEM THAT THEY ARE ZEALOUS FOR GOD, BUT THEIR ZEAL IS NOT BASED ON KNOWLEDGE. SINCE THEY DID NOT KNOW THE RIGHTEOUSNESS THAT COMES FROM GOD AND SOUGHT TO ESTABLISH THEIR OWN, THEY DID NOT SUBMIT TO GOD'S RIGHTEOUSNESS. CHRIST IS THE END OF THE LAW SO THAT THERE MAY BE RIGHTEOUSNESS FOR EVERYONE WHO BELIEVES.

MOSES DESCRIBES IN THIS WAY THE RIGHTEOUSNESS THAT IS BY THE LAW: "THE MAN WHO DOES THESE THINGS WILL LIVE BY THEM." BUT THE RIGHTEOUSNESS THAT IS BY FAITH SAYS: "DO NOT SAY IN YOUR HEART, 'WHO WILL ASCEND INTO HEAVEN?'" (THAT IS, TO BRING CHRIST DOWN) "OR 'WHO WILL DESCEND INTO THE DEEP?'" (THAT IS, TO BRING CHRIST UP FROM THE DEAD). BUT WHAT DOES IT SAY? "THE WORD IS NEAR YOU; IT IS IN YOUR MOUTH AND IN YOUR HEART," THAT IS, THE WORD OF FAITH WE ARE PROCLAIMING: THAT IF YOU CONFESS WITH YOUR MOUTH, "JESUS IS LORD," AND BELIEVE IN YOUR HEART THAT GOD RAISED HIM FROM THE DEAD, YOU WILL BE SAVED. FOR IT IS WITH YOUR HEART

THAT YOU BELIEVE AND ARE JUSTIFIED, AND IT IS
WITH YOUR MOUTH THAT YOU CONFESS AND ARE
SAVED. AS THE SCRIPTURE SAYS, "ANYONE WHO
TRUSTS IN HIM WILL NEVER BE PUT TO SHAME."
FOR THERE IS NO DIFFERENCE BETWEEN JEW AND
GENTILE—THE SAME LORD IS LORD OF ALL AND
RICHLY BLESSES ALL WHO CALL ON HIM, FOR,
"EVERYONE WHO CALLS ON THE NAME OF THE
LORD WILL BE SAVED."

HOW, THEN, CAN THEY CALL ON THE ONE THEY
HAVE NOT BELIEVED IN? AND HOW CAN THEY
BELIEVE IN THE ONE OF WHOM THEY HAVE NOT
HEARD? AND HOW CAN THEY HEAR WITHOUT
SOMEONE PREACHING TO THEM? AND HOW
CAN THEY PREACH UNLESS THEY ARE SENT? AS IT
IS WRITTEN, "HOW BEAUTIFUL ARE THE FEET OF
THOSE WHO BRING GOOD NEWS!"

BUT NOT ALL THE ISRAELITES ACCEPTED THE
GOOD NEWS. FOR ISAIAH SAYS, "LORD, WHO HAS
BELIEVED OUR MESSAGE?" CONSEQUENTLY, FAITH
COMES FROM HEARING THE MESSAGE, AND THE
MESSAGE IS HEARD THROUGH THE WORD OF
CHRIST. BUT I ASK: DID THEY NOT HEAR? OF
COURSE THEY DID:
"THEIR VOICE HAS GONE OUT INTO ALL THE
EARTH,
THEIR WORDS TO THE ENDS OF THE WORLD."
AGAIN I ASK: DID ISRAEL NOT UNDERSTAND?
FIRST, MOSES SAYS,
"I WILL MAKE YOU ENVIOUS BY THOSE WHO ARE
NOT A NATION;
I WILL MAKE YOU ANGRY BY A NATION THAT HAS
NO UNDERSTANDING."
AND ISAIAH BOLDLY SAYS,
"I WAS FOUND BY THOSE WHO DID NOT SEEK ME;

I REVEALED MYSELF TO THOSE WHO DID NOT ASK FOR ME."

BUT CONCERNING ISRAEL HE SAYS,

"ALL DAY LONG I HAVE HELD OUT MY HANDS TO A DISOBEDIENT AND OBSTINATE PEOPLE."

MEDITATE AND ASK JEHOVAH TO OPEN YOUR EYES

WHAT MUST I DO TO INHERIT ETERNAL LIFE?"

UNITY BETWEEN THE ELECT JEWS AND GENTILES
COMES ONLY WITH LOVE FIRST.

"

LUKE 10:25-28
THE PARABLE OF THE GOOD SAMARITAN

ON ONE OCCASION AN EXPERT IN THE LAW
STOOD UP TO TEST JESUS.
"TEACHER," HE ASKED, "WHAT MUST I DO TO
INHERIT ETERNAL LIFE?"

"WHAT IS WRITTEN IN THE LAW?" HE REPLIED.
"HOW DO YOU READ IT?"

HE ANSWERED,
"'LOVE THE LORD YOUR GOD WITH ALL YOUR
HEART
AND
WITH ALL YOUR SOUL
AND
WITH ALL YOUR STRENGTH
AND
WITH ALL YOUR MIND';
AND,
'LOVE YOUR NEIGHBOR AS YOURSELF.'"

"YOU HAVE ANSWERED CORRECTLY," JESUS REPLIED.

"DO THIS AND YOU WILL LIVE."

MEDITATE AND ASK JEHOVAH TO OPEN YOUR EYES

BE OF NOBLE CHARACTER MY BROTHERS AND SISTERS

ACTS 17:11

NOW THE BEREANS WERE OF MORE NOBLE
CHARACTER
THAN THE THESSALONIANS,

FOR THEY RECEIVED THE MESSAGE WITH GREAT
EAGERNESS

AND EXAMINED THE SCRIPTURES

EVERY DAY TO SEE

IF WHAT PAUL SAID WAS TRUE.

IF YOUR LEADERS ARE NOT TELLING YOU THE
TRUTH THEY SHALL FALL
EZEKIEL 17:24

ALL THE TREES OF THE FIELD WILL KNOW THAT I
THE LORD
BRING DOWN THE TALL TREE AND MAKE THE LOW
TREE GROW TALL.
I DRY UP THE GREEN TREE AND MAKE THE DRY
TREE FLOURISH.
"'I THE LORD HAVE SPOKEN, AND I WILL DO IT.'"

MEDITATE AND ASK JEHOVAH TO OPEN YOUR EYES

ODE TO JESUS

OPEN MY EYES JESUS, SO I CAN SEE.

JESUS I NEED YOU NOW.

MY LORD JESUS, I HUNGER AND THURST

FOR YOUR LOVE.

MY LORD JESUS, I HUNGER AND THURST

FOR YOUR PRESENCE.

MY LORD JESUS, I HUNGER AND THURST

FOR YOUR RIGHTEOUSNESS,

I WANT MORE TO SHARE.

MY LORD JESUS, I AM DESPARATE

FOR YOUR MERCY.

MY LORD JESUS, I HAVE A HUNGRY HEART

FOR YOU TO DWELL IN ME,

COME TO ME.

MY LORD JESUS, I AM STARVING FOR YOU,

POUR YOURSELF INTO ME.

MY LORD JESUS, PROVIDE YOUR PROVISIONS

TO ME, SO I CAN FEED OTHERS.

JESUS I NEED YOU NOW.

JEHOVAH I NEED YOU NOW.

HOLY SPIRIT I NEED YOU NOW.

I WANT YOUR LOVE JESUS,

SO I COULD LOVE OTHERS,

JUST LIKE YOU.

MEDITATE AND ASK JEHOVAH TO OPEN YOUR EYES

JESUS GREAT COMMISSION TO HIS JEWISH DISCIPLES AND GENTILE FOLLOWERS

MATTHEW 28:16-20

THEN THE ELEVEN DISCIPLES WENT TO GALILEE,

TO THE MOUNTAIN WHERE JESUS HAD TOLD
THEM TO GO.

WHEN THEY SAW HIM
(JEWS SAW JESUS),

THEY WORSHIPED HIM
(PRAISE GOD ALWAYS);

BUT SOME DOUBTED.

THEN JESUS CAME TO THEM AND SAID,

"ALL AUTHORITY IN HEAVEN AND ON EARTH HAS
BEEN GIVEN TO ME.

(JESUS IS INCHARGE OF ALL AUTHORITY)

THEREFORE

GO AND MAKE DISCIPLES OF ALL NATIONS,

BAPTIZING THEM IN THE NAME OF THE FATHER
AND OF THE SON AND OF THE HOLY SPIRIT,

AND

TEACHING THEM TO OBEY EVERYTHING I HAVE
COMMANDED YOU.

AND SURELY I AM WITH YOU ALWAYS,

TO THE VERY END OF THE AGE."

MEDITATE AND ASK JEHOVAH TO OPEN YOUR EYES

JEHOVAH DO NOT SEE JEWS AND GENTILES DIFFERENT BECAUSE OF RACE

GOD JEHOVAH SEES US BASED ON;

WHETHER WE ACCEPT JESUS AND HIM,
AND
WHETHER WE SIN OR NOT

AMOS 9:7

JEHOVAH SAID,

"ARE NOT YOU ISRAELITES
THE SAME TO ME AS THE CUSHITES?"
DECLARES THE LORD.
"DID I NOT BRING ISRAEL UP FROM EGYPT,
THE PHILISTINES FROM CAPHTOR . . . . . . "
AND THE ARAMEANS FROM KIR?

AMOS 9:10

JEHOVAH SAID,

ALL THE SINNERS AMONG MY PEOPLE
WILL DIE BY THE SWORD,
ALL THOSE WHO SAY,
'DISASTER WILL NOT OVERTAKE OR MEET US.'

PSALM 2:7

SPEAK THROUGH KING DAVID ABOUT JESUS,
JEHOVAH SAID,

"I WILL PROCLAIM THE DECREE OF JEHOVAH:
HE SAID TO JESUS, "YOU ARE MY SON ; TODAY I
HAVE BECOME YOUR FATHER."

MEDITATE AND ASK JEHOVAH TO OPEN YOUR EYES

IS SATAN IN YOUR PLACE OF WORSHIP?

MY QUESTION TO ALL THE ELECT GENTILES AND
JEWS IS, WHO DOES YOUR PASTOR AND
RABBI WORK FOR, JEHOVAH, CHRIST OR SATAN.
MANY PASTORS AND RABBIS ARE SELF CENTERED
AND REFUSE TO ACCEPT THE IDEA OF UNIFYING
THE BODY OF CHRIST, WORLD WIDE.
IF YOUR PASTOR OR RABBI
IS REFUSING TO UNIFY OR JOIN WITH THE TOTAL
BODY OF CHRIST THEN,
HE IS WORKING FOR SATAN
2 CORINTHIANS 11:13-15
PAUL AND THE FALSE APOSTLES

FOR SUCH MEN ARE FALSE APOSTLES, DECEITFUL
WORKMEN, MASQUERADING AS
APOSTLES OF CHRIST. AND NO WONDER, FOR
SATAN HIMSELF MASQUERADES AS AN
ANGEL OF LIGHT. IT IS NOT SURPRISING, THEN, IF
HIS SERVANTS MASQUERADE AS
SERVANTS OF RIGHTEOUSNESS.

THEIR END WILL BE WHAT THEIR ACTIONS
DESERVE.

NOTE, THE ACTS OF THE SINFUL NATURE:

SEXUAL IMMORALITY, IMPURITY, IDOLATRY,
HATRED, DISCORD,

JEALOUSY, FITS OF RAGE, SELFISH AMBITION, DISSENTIONS,

FACTIONS(BETWEEN CHURCHES),

ENVY, DRUNKENNESS AND ORGIES.

NOW, IS YOUR PASTOR OR CHURCH SINNING?

MEDITATE AND ASK JEHOVAH TO OPEN YOUR EYES

ACCORDING TO PAUL SALVATION IS FOR THE JEWS AND GENTILES

ACTS 13:16-33

STANDING UP, PAUL MOTIONED WITH HIS HAND AND SAID: "MEN OF ISRAEL AND YOU GENTILES WHO WORSHIP GOD, LISTEN TO ME! THE GOD OF THE PEOPLE OF ISRAEL CHOSE OUR FATHERS; HE MADE THE PEOPLE PROSPER DURING THEIR STAY IN EGYPT, WITH MIGHTY POWER HE LED THEM OUT OF THAT COUNTRY, HE ENDURED THEIR CONDUCT FOR ABOUT FORTY YEARS IN THE DESERT, HE OVERTHREW SEVEN NATIONS IN CANAAN AND GAVE THEIR LAND TO HIS PEOPLE AS THEIR INHERITANCE. ALL THIS TOOK ABOUT 450 YEARS.

"AFTER THIS, GOD GAVE THEM JUDGES UNTIL THE TIME OF SAMUEL THE PROPHET. THEN THE PEOPLE ASKED FOR A KING, AND HE GAVE THEM SAUL SON OF KISH, OF THE TRIBE OF BENJAMIN, WHO RULED FORTY YEARS. AFTER REMOVING SAUL, HE MADE DAVID THEIR KING. HE TESTIFIED CONCERNING HIM: 'I HAVE FOUND DAVID SON OF JESSE A MAN AFTER MY OWN HEART; HE WILL DO EVERYTHING I WANT HIM TO DO.'

"FROM THIS MAN'S DESCENDANTS GOD HAS BROUGHT TO ISRAEL THE SAVIOR JESUS, AS HE PROMISED. BEFORE THE COMING OF JESUS, JOHN PREACHED REPENTANCE AND BAPTISM TO ALL THE PEOPLE OF ISRAEL. AS JOHN WAS COMPLETING HIS WORK, HE SAID: 'WHO DO YOU THINK I AM? I AM

NOT THAT ONE. NO, BUT HE IS COMING AFTER ME,
WHOSE SANDALS I AM NOT WORTHY TO UNTIE.'
"BROTHERS, CHILDREN OF ABRAHAM, AND YOU
GOD-FEARING GENTILES,
IT IS TO US THAT THIS MESSAGE OF SALVATION HAS
BEEN SENT.

THE PEOPLE OF JERUSALEM AND THEIR RULERS DID
NOT RECOGNIZE JESUS, YET IN CONDEMNING HIM
THEY FULFILLED THE WORDS OF THE PROPHETS
THAT ARE READ EVERY SABBATH. THOUGH THEY
FOUND NO PROPER GROUND FOR A DEATH
SENTENCE, THEY ASKED PILATE TO HAVE HIM
EXECUTED. WHEN THEY HAD CARRIED OUT ALL
THAT WAS WRITTEN ABOUT HIM(JESUS CHRIST),
THEY TOOK HIM DOWN FROM THE TREE AND LAID
HIM IN A TOMB.

BUT GOD RAISED HIM FROM THE DEAD,

AND FOR MANY DAYS HE WAS SEEN
(JESUS WAS SEEN BY JEWS)
BY THOSE WHO HAD TRAVELED WITH HIM FROM
GALILEE TO JERUSALEM.
THEY ARE NOW HIS WITNESSES TO OUR
PEOPLE(JEWS).

PAUL TELLS HIS JEWISH BROTHERS,
"WE TELL YOU THE GOOD NEWS: WHAT GOD
PROMISED OUR FATHERS HE HAS FULFILLED FOR
US,
THEIR CHILDREN, BY RAISING UP JESUS. AS IT IS
WRITTEN IN THE SECOND PSALM:
"'YOU ARE MY SON;
TODAY I HAVE BECOME YOUR FATHER.

MEDITATE AND ASK JEHOVAH TO OPEN YOUR EYES

RICH MAN POOR MAN:

DID YOU EVER REALIZE IN THE FOLLOWING STORY
THAT THE ONLY REQUIREMENT LAZARUS, THE
POOR MAN, HAD
TO ENTER HEAVEN WAS THE FACT THAT HE WAS
POOR.

NOW MOVE LAZARUS' NAME AND
PUT 'LAZARUS FROM AFRICA'.
NOW MOVE THE RICH MAN AND
PUT 'RICH MAN FROM AMERICA'.
IT IS VERY INTERESTING AIN'T IT?
LUKE 16:19-31
THE RICH MAN FROM AMERICA AND LAZARUS
FROM AFRICA
OR
AMERICA AND AFRICA

"THERE WAS A RICH MAN(FROM AMERICA) WHO
WAS DRESSED IN PURPLE AND FINE LINEN AND
LIVED IN LUXURY EVERY DAY. AT HIS GATE WAS
LAID A BEGGAR NAMED LAZARUS(FROM AFRICA),
COVERED WITH SORES AND LONGING TO EAT
WHAT FELL FROM THE RICH MAN'S TABLE. EVEN
THE DOGS CAME AND LICKED HIS SORES.

"THE TIME CAME WHEN THE BEGGAR FROM AFRICA
DIED AND THE ANGELS CARRIED HIM TO ABRAHAM'S
SIDE. THE RICH MAN FROM AMERICA ALSO DIED
AND WAS BURIED. IN HELL, WHERE HE WAS IN
TORMENT, HE LOOKED UP AND SAW ABRAHAM FAR

AWAY, WITH THE BEGGAR LAZARUS, FROM AFRICA, BY HIS SIDE. SO THE RICH MAN FROM AMERICA CALLED TO HIM, 'FATHER ABRAHAM, HAVE PITY ON ME AND SEND LAZARUS FROM AFRICA TO DIP THE TIP OF HIS FINGER IN WATER AND COOL MY TONGUE, BECAUSE I AM IN AGONY IN THIS FIRE.'

"BUT ABRAHAM REPLIED, 'SON, REMEMBER THAT IN YOUR LIFETIME YOU RECEIVED YOUR GOOD THINGS, WHILE LAZARUS FROM AFRICA RECEIVED BAD THINGS, BUT NOW HE IS COMFORTED HERE AND YOU ARE IN AGONY. AND BESIDES ALL THIS, BETWEEN US AND YOU A GREAT CHASM HAS BEEN FIXED, SO THAT THOSE WHO WANT TO GO FROM HERE TO YOU CANNOT, NOR CAN ANYONE CROSS OVER FROM THERE TO US.'
" THE RICH MAN FROM AMERICA ANSWERED, 'THEN I BEG YOU, FATHER, SEND LAZARUS FROM AFRICA TO MY FATHER'S HOUSE, FOR I HAVE FIVE BROTHERS. LET HIM WARN THEM, SO THAT THEY WILL NOT ALSO COME TO THIS PLACE OF TORMENT.'
"ABRAHAM REPLIED, 'THEY HAVE PASTORS AND PROPHETS; LET THEM LISTEN TO THEM.'
"'NO, FATHER ABRAHAM,' THE RICH MAN FROM AMERICA SAID, 'BUT IF SOMEONE FROM THE DEAD GOES TO THEM, THEY WILL REPENT.'
"HE SAID TO HIM, 'IF THEY DO NOT LISTEN TO THE PASTORS AND THE PROPHETS, THEY WILL NOT BE CONVINCED EVEN IF SOMEONE RISES FROM THE DEAD.'"

MEDITATE AND ASK JEHOVAH TO OPEN YOUR EYES

JEHOVAH WILL BE PROUD OF AFRICA

AFRICA WILL BE LIKE EDEN

AFRICA WILL PLEASE JEHOVAH
ZEPHANIAH 3:10-13

FROM BEYOND THE RIVERS OF CUSH(AFRICA)
MY WORSHIPERS, MY SCATTERED PEOPLE,
WILL BRING ME OFFERINGS.(JUST LIKE THE MAGI
AT JESUS' BIRTH)

ON THAT DAY(THE DAY JESUS RETURNS) YOU WILL
NOT BE PUT TO SHAME
FOR ALL THE WRONGS YOU HAVE DONE TO ME,
BECAUSE I WILL REMOVE FROM THIS CITY

THOSE WHO REJOICE IN THEIR PRIDE.
NEVER AGAIN WILL YOU BE HAUGHTY
ON MY HOLY HILL.

BUT I WILL LEAVE WITHIN YOU
THE MEEK AND HUMBLE,
WHO TRUST IN THE NAME OF THE LORD.

THE REMNANT OF ISRAEL WILL DO NO WRONG;
THEY WILL SPEAK NO LIES,
NOR WILL DECEIT BE FOUND IN THEIR MOUTHS.

THEY WILL EAT AND LIE DOWN
AND NO ONE WILL MAKE THEM AFRAID."

MEDITATE AND ASK JEHOVAH TO OPEN YOUR EYES

A VISION FROM JEHOVAH ABOUT AFRICA

LUKE 15:11-32
JESUS PARABLE OF THE LOST SON
(ISRAEL AND HIS OLDER BROTHER AFRICA)

JESUS CONTINUED: "THERE WAS A MAN WHO HAD TWO SONS.(AFRICA & ISRAEL) THE YOUNGER ONE(ISRAEL) SAID TO HIS FATHER, 'FATHER, GIVE ME MY SHARE OF THE ESTATE.' SO HE DIVIDED HIS PROPERTY BETWEEN THEM.
"NOT LONG AFTER THAT, THE YOUNGER SON GOT TOGETHER ALL HE HAD, SET OFF FOR A DISTANT COUNTRY AND THERE SQUANDERED HIS WEALTH IN WILD LIVING. AFTER HE HAD SPENT EVERYTHING, THERE WAS A SEVERE FAMINE(TOUGH TIMES) IN THAT WHOLE COUNTRY, AND HE BEGAN TO BE IN NEED. SO HE WENT AND HIRED HIMSELF OUT TO A CITIZEN OF THAT COUNTRY, WHO SENT HIM TO HIS FIELDS TO FEED PIGS. HE LONGED TO FILL HIS STOMACH WITH THE PODS THAT THE PIGS WERE EATING, BUT NO ONE GAVE HIM ANYTHING.

"WHEN HE CAME TO HIS SENSES, HE SAID, 'HOW MANY OF MY FATHER'S(JEHOVAH) HIRED MEN HAVE FOOD TO SPARE, AND HERE I AM STARVING TO DEATH! I WILL SET OUT AND GO BACK TO MY FATHER AND SAY TO HIM: FATHER(JEHOVAH), I HAVE SINNED AGAINST HEAVEN AND AGAINST YOU. I AM NO LONGER WORTHY TO BE CALLED YOUR SON;

MAKE ME LIKE ONE OF YOUR HIRED MEN.' SO HE
GOT UP AND WENT TO HIS FATHER.
"BUT WHILE HE WAS STILL A LONG WAY OFF,
HIS FATHER SAW HIM AND WAS FILLED WITH
COMPASSION FOR HIM; HE RAN TO HIS SON, THREW
HIS ARMS AROUND HIM AND KISSED HIM.
"THE SON SAID TO HIM, 'FATHER, I HAVE SINNED
AGAINST HEAVEN AND AGAINST YOU. I AM NO
LONGER WORTHY TO BE CALLED YOUR SON.'
"BUT THE FATHER SAID TO HIS SERVANTS, 'QUICK!
BRING THE BEST ROBE AND PUT IT ON HIM. PUT
A RING ON HIS FINGER AND SANDALS ON HIS
FEET. BRING THE FATTENED CALF AND KILL IT. LET'S
HAVE A FEAST AND CELEBRATE. FOR THIS SON OF
MINE WAS DEAD(ETERNAL DEATH) AND IS ALIVE
AGAIN(ETERNAL LIFE); HE WAS LOST AND IS FOUND.'
SO THEY BEGAN TO CELEBRATE.
"MEANWHILE, THE OLDER SON(AFRICA) WAS IN THE
FIELD. WHEN HE CAME NEAR THE HOUSE, HE HEARD
MUSIC AND DANCING. SO HE CALLED ONE OF THE
SERVANTS AND ASKED HIM WHAT WAS GOING ON.
'YOUR BROTHER HAS COME,' HE REPLIED, 'AND YOUR
FATHER HAS KILLED THE FATTENED CALF BECAUSE
HE HAS HIM BACK SAFE AND SOUND(MERCIFUL
JEHOVAH).'

"THE OLDER BROTHER(AFRICA DON'T WANT TO
HELP OR CELEBRATE) BECAME ANGRY AND REFUSED
TO GO IN. SO HIS FATHER WENT OUT AND PLEADED
WITH HIM. BUT HE ANSWERED HIS FATHER,
'LOOK! ALL THESE YEARS I'VE BEEN SLAVING FOR
YOU(AFRICA NEVER GAVE UP ON JEHOVAH) AND
NEVER DISOBEYED(JEHOVAH LOVE OBEDIENCE)
YOUR ORDERS. YET YOU NEVER GAVE ME EVEN A
YOUNG GOAT SO I COULD CELEBRATE WITH MY
FRIENDS(AFRICA SUFFERED FOR JEHOVAH). BUT
WHEN THIS SON(ISRAEL) OF YOURS WHO HAS
SQUANDERED YOUR PROPERTY WITH PROSTITUTES

COMES HOME, YOU KILL THE FATTENED CALF FOR HIM!'

"'MY SON(AFRICA),' THE FATHER(JEHOVAH) SAID, 'YOU ARE ALWAYS WITH ME, AND EVERYTHING I HAVE IS YOURS. BUT WE HAD TO CELEBRATE AND BE GLAD, BECAUSE THIS BROTHER(ISRAEL) OF YOURS WAS DEAD(ETERNAL DAMNATION) AND IS ALIVE AGAIN(SAVED); HE WAS LOST AND IS FOUND.'"

MEDITATE AND ASK JEHOVAH TO OPEN YOUR EYES

ISRAEL WILL NOT LOOSE THEIR LAND

ISRAEL WILL NOT EVER BE DESTROYED TOTALLY

AMOS 9:11-15
ISRAEL'S RESTORATION

"IN THAT DAY I WILL RESTORE
DAVID'S FALLEN TENT.

I WILL REPAIR ITS BROKEN PLACES,
RESTORE ITS RUINS,
AND BUILD IT AS IT USED TO BE,

SO THAT THEY MAY POSSESS THE REMNANT OF
EDOM
AND ALL THE NATIONS THAT BEAR MY NAME,"
DECLARES THE LORD, WHO WILL DO THESE
THINGS.

"THE DAYS ARE COMING," DECLARES THE LORD,
"WHEN THE REAPER WILL BE OVERTAKEN BY THE
PLOWMAN
AND THE PLANTER BY THE ONE TREADING
GRAPES.
NEW WINE WILL DRIP FROM THE MOUNTAINS
AND FLOW FROM ALL THE HILLS.

JEHOVAH SAID,"I WILL . . . ."

I WILL BRING BACK MY EXILED PEOPLE ISRAEL;

THEY WILL

THEY WILL REBUILD THE RUINED CITIES AND
LIVE IN THEM.
THEY WILL PLANT VINEYARDS AND DRINK
THEIR WINE;
THEY WILL MAKE GARDENS AND EAT THEIR FRUIT.
JEHOVAH WILL

JEHOVAH WILL PLANT ISRAEL IN THEIR OWN
LAND,
NEVER AGAIN TO BE UPROOTED
FROM THE LAND I HAVE GIVEN THEM,"

MEDITATE AND ASK JEHOVAH TO OPEN YOUR EYES

THE PARABLE OF THE PHARISEE

LUKE 18:9-14
(PASTORS AND RABBIS)
AND THE TAX COLLECTOR
(ALL OTHER SINNERS)

TO SOME WHO WERE CONFIDENT OF THEIR OWN RIGHTEOUSNESS(PASTORS AND RABBIS) AND LOOKED DOWN ON EVERYBODY
ELSE, JESUS TOLD THIS PARABLE: "TWO MEN WENT UP TO THE TEMPLE TO PRAY, ONE A PHARISEE AND THE OTHER A TAX COLLECTOR.
THE PHARISEE STOOD UP AND PRAYED ABOUT HIMSELF: 'GOD, I THANK YOU THAT I AM NOT LIKE OTHER MEN—ROBBERS,
EVILDOERS, ADULTERERS—OR EVEN LIKE THIS TAX COLLECTOR. I FAST TWICE A WEEK AND GIVE A TENTH OF ALL I GET
(SAD TO SAY, MOST PASTORS AND RABBIS TODAY ARE NOT HUMBLE).'
"BUT THE TAX COLLECTOR STOOD AT A DISTANCE. HE WOULD NOT EVEN LOOK UP TO HEAVEN
(HUMBLE AND FEELING UNWORTHY OF ANY GRACE),
BUT BEAT HIS BREAST AND SAID, 'GOD, HAVE MERCY ON ME, A SINNER.
(SIMPLE PRAYER, HE TOOK RESPONSIBILITY FOR HIS OWN BEHAVIOR, NO EXCUSES, NO COMPLAINTS AND COMPARED HIMSELF TO NO ONE. LIKE ZACCHAEUS HE WAS OPEN TO CHANGING HIS LIFE, RIGHT NOW.)'

"I TELL YOU THAT THIS MAN, RATHER THAN THE OTHER, WENT HOME JUSTIFIED BEFORE GOD.

FOR EVERYONE WHO EXALTS HIMSELF WILL BE HUMBLED, AND HE WHO HUMBLES HIMSELF WILL BE EXALTED."

MEDITATE AND ASK JEHOVAH TO OPEN YOUR EYES

HELPS US UNDERSTAND THE PROCEDURE BEFORE JESUS RETURNS

MOSES AT MOUNT SINAI:
EXODUS 19:3-22

3 THEN MOSES WENT UP TO GOD, AND THE LORD CALLED TO HIM FROM THE MOUNTAIN AND SAID, "THIS IS WHAT YOU ARE TO SAY TO THE HOUSE OF JACOB(12 TRIBES) AND WHAT YOU ARE TO TELL THE PEOPLE OF ISRAEL(12 TRIBES): 4 'YOU YOURSELVES HAVE SEEN WHAT I DID TO EGYPT, AND HOW I CARRIED YOU ON EAGLES' WINGS AND BROUGHT YOU TO MYSELF. 5 NOW IF YOU OBEY ME FULLY AND KEEP MY COVENANT, THEN OUT OF ALL NATIONS YOU WILL BE MY TREASURED POSSESSION. ALTHOUGH THE WHOLE EARTH IS MINE, 6 YOU WILL BE FOR ME A KINGDOM OF PRIESTS AND A HOLY NATION(12 TRIBES).' THESE ARE THE WORDS YOU ARE TO SPEAK TO THE ISRAELITES(12 TRIBES)."
7 SO MOSES WENT BACK AND SUMMONED THE ELDERS OF THE PEOPLE AND SET BEFORE THEM ALL THE WORDS THE LORD HAD COMMANDED HIM TO SPEAK. 8 THE PEOPLE ALL RESPONDED TOGETHER, "WE WILL DO EVERYTHING THE LORD HAS SAID." SO MOSES BROUGHT THEIR ANSWER BACK TO THE LORD.
9 THE LORD SAID TO MOSES, "I AM GOING TO COME TO YOU IN A DENSE CLOUD, (SO THAT THE PEOPLE WILL HEAR ME SPEAKING WITH YOU AND WILL

ALWAYS PUT THEIR TRUST IN YOU)." THEN MOSES TOLD THE LORD WHAT THE PEOPLE HAD SAID.

10 AND THE LORD SAID TO MOSES, "GO TO THE PEOPLE AND CONSECRATE THEM(MAKE THEM HOLY) TODAY AND TOMORROW. HAVE THEM WASH THEIR CLOTHES 11 AND BE READY BY THE THIRD DAY(GOD HEAD), BECAUSE ON THAT DAY THE LORD WILL COME DOWN ON MOUNT SINAI IN THE SIGHT OF ALL THE PEOPLE. 12 PUT LIMITS FOR THE PEOPLE AROUND THE MOUNTAIN AND TELL THEM, 'BE CAREFUL THAT YOU DO NOT GO UP THE MOUNTAIN OR TOUCH THE FOOT OF IT. WHOEVER TOUCHES THE MOUNTAIN SHALL SURELY BE PUT TO DEATH. 13 HE SHALL SURELY BE STONED OR SHOT WITH ARROWS; NOT A HAND IS TO BE LAID ON HIM. WHETHER MAN OR ANIMAL, HE SHALL NOT BE PERMITTED TO LIVE.' ONLY WHEN THE (RAM'S HORN SOUNDS) A LONG BLAST MAY THEY GO UP TO THE MOUNTAIN."

14 AFTER MOSES HAD GONE DOWN THE MOUNTAIN TO THE PEOPLE, HE CONSECRATED THEM(MAKE THEM HOLY), AND THEY WASHED THEIR CLOTHES. 15 THEN HE SAID TO THE PEOPLE, "PREPARE YOURSELVES FOR THE THIRD DAY. ABSTAIN FROM SEXUAL RELATIONS."

16 ON THE MORNING OF THE THIRD DAY THERE WAS THUNDER AND LIGHTNING, WITH A THICK CLOUD OVER THE MOUNTAIN, AND A VERY LOUD TRUMPET BLAST. EVERYONE IN THE CAMP TREMBLED. 17 THEN MOSES LED THE PEOPLE OUT OF THE CAMP TO MEET WITH GOD, AND THEY STOOD AT THE FOOT OF THE MOUNTAIN. 18 MOUNT SINAI WAS COVERED WITH SMOKE, BECAUSE THE LORD DESCENDED ON IT IN FIRE. THE SMOKE BILLOWED UP FROM IT LIKE SMOKE FROM A FURNACE, THE WHOLE MOUNTAIN TREMBLED VIOLENTLY, 19 AND THE SOUND OF THE TRUMPET GREW LOUDER AND

LOUDER. THEN MOSES SPOKE AND THE VOICE OF GOD ANSWERED HIM.

20 THE LORD DESCENDED TO THE TOP OF MOUNT SINAI AND CALLED MOSES TO THE TOP OF THE MOUNTAIN. SO MOSES WENT UP 21 AND THE LORD SAID TO HIM, "GO DOWN AND WARN THE PEOPLE SO THEY DO NOT FORCE THEIR WAY THROUGH TO SEE THE LORD AND MANY OF THEM PERISH. 22 EVEN THE PRIESTS, WHO APPROACH THE LORD, MUST CONSECRATE(MAKE THEMSELVES HOLY) THEMSELVES, OR THE LORD WILL BREAK OUT AGAINST THEM."

MEDITATE AND ASK JEHOVAH TO OPEN YOUR EYES

ESPECIALLY WHILE IN WORSHIP.

PSALM 100

A PSALM. FOR GIVING THANKS.

SHOUT FOR JOY TO THE LORD, ALL THE EARTH.

WORSHIP THE LORD WITH GLADNESS;

COME BEFORE HIM WITH JOYFUL SONGS.

KNOW THAT THE LORD IS GOD.

IT IS HE WHO MADE US, AND WE ARE HIS;

WE ARE HIS PEOPLE, THE SHEEP OF HIS PASTURE.

ENTER HIS GATES WITH THANKSGIVING

AND HIS COURTS WITH PRAISE;

GIVE THANKS TO HIM AND PRAISE HIS NAME.

FOR THE LORD IS GOOD AND HIS LOVE ENDURES
FOREVER;

HIS FAITHFULNESS CONTINUES THROUGH ALL
GENERATIONS

MEDITATE AND ASK JEHOVAH TO OPEN YOUR EYES

WE JUST HAVE TO FOLLOW GOD'S WORSHIP INSTRUCTIONS

PSALM 148

PRAISE THE LORD.
PRAISE THE LORD FROM THE HEAVENS;
PRAISE HIM IN THE HEIGHTS ABOVE.
PRAISE HIM, ALL HIS ANGELS;
PRAISE HIM, ALL HIS HEAVENLY HOSTS.
PRAISE HIM, SUN AND MOON;
PRAISE HIM, ALL YOU SHINING STARS.
PRAISE HIM, YOU HIGHEST HEAVENS
AND YOU WATERS ABOVE THE SKIES.

LET THEM PRAISE THE NAME OF THE LORD,
FOR AT HIS COMMAND THEY WERE CREATED,
AND HE ESTABLISHED THEM FOR EVER AND
EVER—
HE ISSUED A DECREE THAT WILL NEVER PASS AWAY.

PRAISE THE LORD FROM THE EARTH,
YOU GREAT SEA CREATURES AND ALL OCEAN
DEPTHS,
LIGHTNING AND HAIL, SNOW AND CLOUDS,
STORMY WINDS THAT DO HIS BIDDING,
YOU MOUNTAINS AND ALL HILLS,
FRUIT TREES AND ALL CEDARS,
WILD ANIMALS AND ALL CATTLE,
SMALL CREATURES AND FLYING BIRDS,
KINGS OF THE EARTH AND ALL NATIONS,
YOU PRINCES AND ALL RULERS ON EARTH,
YOUNG MEN AND WOMEN,
OLD MEN AND CHILDREN.

LET THEM PRAISE THE NAME OF THE LORD,
FOR HIS NAME ALONE IS EXALTED;
HIS SPLENDOR IS ABOVE THE EARTH AND THE
HEAVENS.
AND HE HAS RAISED UP FOR HIS PEOPLE A HORN,
THE PRAISE OF ALL HIS FAITHFUL SERVANTS,
OF ISRAEL, THE PEOPLE CLOSE TO HIS HEART.

PRAISE THE LORD.

MEDITATE AND ASK JEHOVAH TO OPEN YOUR EYES

PSALM 91

1 I WILL DWELL IN THE SHELTER OF THE MOST
HIGH GOD, JEHOVAH
SO I WILL REST IN THE SHADOW OF THE
ALMIGHTY JEHOVAH GOD.

2 I WILL SAY, JEHOVAH, "HE IS MY REFUGE AND MY
FORTRESS,
MY GOD, IN WHOM I TRUST."
3 SURELY HE WILL SAVE ME
FROM THE FOWLER'S SNARE
AND FROM THE DEADLY PESTILENCE.

4 HE WILL COVER ME WITH HIS FEATHERS,
AND UNDER HIS WINGS I WILL FIND REFUGE;
HIS FAITHFULNESS WILL BE MY SHIELD AND
RAMPART.

5 I WILL NOT FEAR THE TERROR OF NIGHT,
NOR THE ARROW THAT FLIES BY DAY,
6 NOR THE PESTILENCE THAT STALKS IN THE
DARKNESS,
NOR THE PLAGUE THAT DESTROYS AT MIDDAY.

7 A THOUSAND MAY FALL AT MY SIDE,
TEN THOUSAND AT MY RIGHT HAND,
BUT IT WILL NOT COME NEAR ME.

8 I WILL ONLY OBSERVE WITH MY EYES
AND SEE THE PUNISHMENT OF THE WICKED.
9 IF I SAY, "JEHOVAH IS MY REFUGE,"
AND I MAKE THE MOST HIGH MY DWELLING,

10 NO HARM WILL OVERTAKE ME,
NO DISASTER WILL COME NEAR MY HOME.
11 FOR JEHOVAH WILL COMMAND HIS ANGELS
CONCERNING ME
TO GUARD ME IN ALL MY WAYS;

12 THE ANGELS WILL LIFT ME UP IN THEIR HANDS,
SO THAT I WILL NOT STRIKE MY FOOT AGAINST A STONE.
13 I WILL TREAD ON THE GREAT LION AND THE COBRA;
I WILL TRAMPLE THE GREAT LION AND THE SERPENT.
14 "BECAUSE HE LOVES ME," SAYS JEHOVAH, "I WILL
RESCUE HIM;
I WILL PROTECT HIM, FOR HE ACKNOWLEDGES MY
NAME, JEHOVAH.
15 HE WILL CALL ON ME, JEHOVAH AND I WILL
ANSWER HIM;
I WILL BE WITH HIM IN TROUBLE,
I WILL DELIVER HIM AND HONOR HIM.
16 WITH LONG LIFE I WILL SATISFY HIM AND
SHOW HIM MY SALVATION."

MEDITATE AND ASK JEHOVAH TO OPEN YOUR EYES

PSALM 91

1 I WILL LIVE IN THE SHELTER OF THE MOST HIGH
GOD, JESUS.
I WILL FIND REST IN THE SHADOW OF THE
ALMIGHTY, JESUS.
2 THIS I DECLARE ABOUT MY GOD, JESUS:
HE ALONE IS MY REFUGE, MY PLACE OF SAFETY;
HE IS MY GOD, AND I TRUST HIM.
3 FOR HE WILL RESCUE ME FROM EVERY TRAP
AND PROTECT ME FROM ALL SATAN PLANS AND
HIS EVIL DEADLY DISEASES.
4 HE WILL COVER ME WITH HIS FEATHERS.
HE WILL SHELTER ME WITH HIS WINGS.
HIS FAITHFUL PROMISES ARE MY ARMOR AND
PROTECTION.
5 I WILL NOT BE AFRAID OF THE TERRORS OF THE
NIGHT,
NOR THE ARROW THAT FLIES IN THE DAY.
6 I WILL NOT DREAD THE DISEASES THAT STALKS
IN THE DARKNESS OF LIFE,
NOR THE DISASTERS THAT STRIKES AT MIDDAY.
7 THOUGH A THOUSAND MAY FALL AT MY SIDE,
THOUGH TEN THOUSAND ARE AROUND ME,
THE EVILS OF THIS WORLD WILL NOT EVER
TOUCH ME.
8 I WILL JUST OPEN MY EYES,
AND SEE HOW THE WICKED ARE PUNISHED.

9 WHEN I MAKE THE LORD, JESUS MY REFUGE,
WHEN I MAKE THE MOST HIGH, JESUS MY
SHELTER,

10 NO EVIL WILL EVER COME NEAR ME;
NO PLAGUE WILL EVER COME NEAR MY HOME.
11 FOR JESUS WILL ORDER HIS ANGELS
TO PROTECT ME AND MY FAMILY WHEREVER I GO.
12 JESUS' ANGELS WILL HOLD ME UP WITH THEIR
HANDS
SO I WON'T EVEN HURT MY FOOT ON A STONE.
13 I WILL TRAMPLE UPON LIONS AND COBRAS;
I WILL CRUSH FIERCE LIONS AND SERPENTS
UNDER MY FEET!
14 THE LORD JESUS SAYS, "I WILL RESCUE ALL WHO
LOVE ME.
I WILL PROTECT ALL WHO TRUST IN MY NAME,
JESUS.
15 WHEN HE CALL ON ME, JESUS, I WILL ANSWER
HIM;
I WILL BE WITH HE WHO IS IN TROUBLE.
I WILL RESCUE AND HONOR HIM WHO IS IN
TROUBLE.
16 I WILL REWARD HIM WHO WAS IN TROUBLE
WITH A LONG LIFE
AND GIVE HIM MY SALVATION."

MEDITATE AND ASK JEHOVAH TO OPEN YOUR EYES

FULL ARMOR OF GOD:

EPHESIANS 6

BE STRONG IN THE LORD JEHOVAH AND IN HIS MIGHTY POWER.

PUT ON THE FULL ARMOR OF GOD JEHOVAH,

SO THAT I CAN TAKE MY STAND AGAINST THE DEVIL'S SCHEMES.

FOR MY STRUGGLE IS NOT AGAINST FLESH AND BLOOD,

BUT AGAINST THE RULERS, AGAINST THE AUTHORITIES,

AGAINST THE POWERS OF THIS DARK WORLD AND

AGAINST THE SPIRITUAL FORCES OF EVIL IN THE HEAVENLY REALMS.

THEREFORE

PUT ON THE FULL ARMOR OF GOD JEHOVAH, SO THAT WHEN THE DAY OF EVIL COMES,

I MAY BE ABLE TO STAND MY GROUND,

AND

AFTER I HAVE DONE EVERYTHING, TO STAND.

STAND FIRM THEN I WILL, WITH THE BELT OF
TRUTH BUCKLED AROUND MY WAIST,

WITH THE BREASTPLATE OF RIGHTEOUSNESS IN
PLACE,

AND

WITH MY FEET FITTED WITH THE READINESS THAT
COMES FROM THE GOSPEL OF PEACE.
IN ADDITION TO ALL THIS,

TAKE UP THE SHIELD OF FAITH,

WITH WHICH I CAN EXTINGUISH ALL THE
FLAMING ARROWS OF THE EVIL ONE.

TAKE THE HELMET OF SALVATION

AND

THE SWORD OF THE SPIRIT,

WHICH IS THE WORD OF GOD.

MEDITATE AND ASK JEHOVAH TO OPEN YOUR EYES

SHOULD WOMEN BE PASTORS OR PRIEST IN THE CHURCH?

I SAY AN ABSOLUTE, YES.

JEHOVAH IS A GOD OF AUTHORITY AND ORDER, ALL WHO WOULD BELIEVE IN CHRIST WAS PLACED ON THE SAME LEVEL AS PRIEST(MEN AND WOMEN). OUT OF THE PRIEST SOME(MEN AND WOMEN) ARE CHOSEN TO PREACH AS PASTORS.

JESUS DEATH AND RESURRECTION MADE ALL MANKIND WHO BELIEVE IN HIM, A KINGDOM OF PRIEST, WITH HIM BEING THE HIGH PRIEST. THUS, WE(MEN AND WOMEN) ALL CAN NOW ENTER THAT MOST HOLY PLACE. EVEN THE ANGELS IN HEAVEN ACKNOWLEDGES US(MEN AND WOMEN) AS PRIEST. THE GREAT COMMISSION WAS GIVEN BY JESUS TO THE DISCIPLES TO BAPTIZE EVERYONE, MEN AND WOMEN. THIS MAKES ALL BELIEVERS TEACHERS.

HEBREWS 3:1

THEREFORE, HOLY BROTHERS AND SISTERS, WHO SHARE IN THE HEAVENLY CALLING, FIX YOUR THOUGHTS ON JESUS, WHOM WE ACKNOWLEDGE AS OUR APOSTLE AND HIGH PRIEST.

REVELATION 5:9-10

AND THEY SANG A NEW SONG:
"YOU ARE WORTHY TO TAKE THE SCROLL
AND TO OPEN ITS SEALS,
BECAUSE YOU WERE SLAIN,
AND WITH YOUR BLOOD YOU PURCHASED
MEN(AND WOMEN) FOR GOD
FROM EVERY TRIBE AND LANGUAGE AND PEOPLE
AND NATION.
YOU HAVE MADE THEM(MEN AND WOMEN) TO BE A
KINGDOM AND PRIESTS TO SERVE OUR GOD,
AND THEY(MEN AND WOMEN) WILL REIGN ON
THE EARTH."
HEBREWS 10:11-13

DAY AFTER DAY EVERY PRIEST STANDS AND
PERFORMS HIS RELIGIOUS DUTIES; AGAIN AND
AGAIN HE OFFERS THE SAME SACRIFICES, WHICH
CAN NEVER TAKE AWAY SINS. 12 BUT WHEN THIS
PRIEST HAD OFFERED FOR ALL TIME ONE SACRIFICE
FOR SINS, HE SAT DOWN AT THE RIGHT HAND OF
GOD, 13 AND SINCE THAT TIME HE WAITS FOR HIS
ENEMIES TO BE MADE HIS FOOTSTOOL.

HEBREWS 10:19-21

THEREFORE, BROTHERS AND SISTERS, SINCE WE
HAVE CONFIDENCE TO ENTER THE MOST HOLY
PLACE BY THE BLOOD OF JESUS, 20 BY A NEW AND
LIVING WAY OPENED FOR US THROUGH THE
CURTAIN, THAT IS, HIS BODY, 21 AND SINCE WE
HAVE A GREAT PRIEST OVER THE HOUSE OF GOD,

MATTHEW 28:19-20

THEREFORE GO AND MAKE DISCIPLES OF ALL NATIONS, BAPTIZING THEM IN THE NAME OF THE FATHER AND OF THE SON AND OF THE HOLY SPIRIT, 20 AND TEACHING THEM(MEN AND WOMEN) TO OBEY EVERYTHING I HAVE COMMANDED YOU. AND SURELY I AM WITH YOU ALWAYS, TO THE VERY END OF THE AGE."

MEDITATE AND ASK JEHOVAH TO OPEN YOUR EYES

DO NOT WORSHIP ANGELS.

THEY ARE JUST LIKE US.

REVELATION 19:9-10
THEN THE ANGEL SAID TO ME, "WRITE:
'BLESSED ARE THOSE WHO ARE INVITED TO THE
WEDDING SUPPER OF THE LAMB!'"
AND HE ADDED, "THESE ARE THE TRUE WORDS OF
GOD."

AT THIS I FELL AT HIS FEET TO WORSHIP HIM. BUT
HE SAID TO ME, "DO NOT DO IT!

I AM A FELLOW SERVANT WITH YOU AND WITH
YOUR BROTHERS WHO HOLD TO THE TESTIMONY
OF JESUS.

WORSHIP JEHOVAH!

FOR THE TESTIMONY OF JESUS IS THE SPIRIT OF
PROPHECY."

MEDITATE AND ASK JEHOVAH TO OPEN YOUR EYES

GENTILES WILL JUDGE JEWS, JEWS WILL JUDGE GENTILES

MATTHEW 19:28

JESUS SAID TO THEM, "I TELL YOU THE TRUTH AT THE RENEWAL OF ALL THINGS, (WHEN JESUS RETURNS A SECOND TIME AT THE RIGHT HAND OF JEHOVAH) WHEN THE SON OF MAN SITS ON HIS GLORIOUS THRONE,YOU

(JEWS AND GENTILES)

WHO HAVE FOLLOWED MEWILL ALSO SIT ON TWELVE THRONES,

JUDGING THE TWELVE TRIBES OF ISRAEL.

MEDITATE AND ASK JEHOVAH TO OPEN YOUR EYES

THIS IS A PROPHETIC WORD OF KNOWLEDGE FOR ME:

"HAVE I FALLEN ASLEEP, " SAITH THE LORD JEHOVAH, "OR

DO I NO LONGER HAVE THE POWER THAT I USED

TO CREATE THE UNIVERSE AND EVERY BREATHING

CREATURE? NO! I AM THE GOD OF THE IMPOSSIBLE!

THERE IS NOTHING TOO HARD FOR ME TO DO. I

WOULD HAVE YOU PLACE THIS SITUATION THAT IS

CONCERNING YOU INTO MY HANDS AND LEAVE IT

THERE. GIVE ME CONTROL OF IT AND OF ALL OF

YOUR LIFE. I WILL TAKE CARE OF YOU. DO NOT

DOUBT THAT I WILL GIVE YOU WHAT YOU NEED . . . .

AND MORE TO BLESS YOU! I DELIGHT IN YOU. I WILL

TURN YOUR PROBLEMS INTO MIRACLES AS YOU GIVE ME

ACCESS INTO EVERY AREA OF YOUR LIFE AND MAKE

ME YOUR LORD. DO NOT HOLD BACK YOUR TITHES

AND OFFERINGS FROM ME! GIVE, AND YOU WILL RECEIVE."

MEDITATE AND ASK JEHOVAH TO OPEN YOUR EYES

UNITY IN THE ELECT FAMILY, JEWS AND GENTILES WILL NOT BE POSSIBLE WITHOUT LOVE AND ORGANIZATION.

1 CORINTHIANS 13

LOVE

LOVE IS PATIENT,
LOVE IS KIND.
IT DOES NOT ENVY,
IT DOES NOT BOAST,
IT IS NOT PROUD.
IT DOES NOT DISHONOR OTHERS,
IT IS NOT SELF-SEEKING,
IT IS NOT EASILY ANGERED,
IT KEEPS NO RECORD OF WRONGS.
LOVE DOES NOT DELIGHT IN EVIL
BUT REJOICES WITH THE TRUTH.
IT ALWAYS PROTECTS,
ALWAYS TRUSTS,
ALWAYS HOPES,
ALWAYS PERSEVERES.
LOVE NEVER FAILS.

JOHN 13:34-35

JESUS SAID,
"A NEW COMMAND I GIVE YOU: LOVE ONE
ANOTHER. AS I HAVE LOVED YOU, SO YOU MUST
LOVE ONE ANOTHER. BY THIS EVERYONE WILL

KNOW THAT YOU ARE MY DISCIPLES, IF YOU LOVE
ONE ANOTHER."

JOHN 15:16-17

YOU DID NOT CHOOSE ME, BUT I CHOSE YOU
AND APPOINTED YOU SO THAT YOU MIGHT GO
AND BEAR FRUIT—FRUIT THAT WILL LAST—AND
SO THAT WHATEVER YOU ASK IN MY NAME THE
FATHER WILL GIVE YOU. THIS IS MY COMMAND:
LOVE EACH OTHER.

MEDITATE AND ASK JEHOVAH TO OPEN YOUR EYES

LOVE AND ROMANS

ROMANS 12:9-21

LOVE MUST BE SINCERE. HATE WHAT IS EVIL;
CLING TO WHAT IS GOOD.
BE DEVOTED TO ONE ANOTHER IN BROTHERLY
LOVE.
(ALL BELIEVERS ARE TO BE DEVOTED TO
EACHOTHER)
HONOR ONE ANOTHER ABOVE YOURSELVES.
NEVER BE LACKING IN ZEAL, BUT KEEP YOUR
SPIRITUAL FERVOR, SERVING THE LORD.
BE JOYFUL IN HOPE, PATIENT IN AFFLICTION,
FAITHFUL IN PRAYER.
SHARE WITH GOD'S PEOPLE WHO ARE IN NEED.
PRACTICE HOSPITALITY.
BLESS THOSE WHO PERSECUTE YOU; BLESS AND DO
NOT CURSE.
REJOICE WITH THOSE WHO REJOICE; MOURN
WITH THOSE WHO MOURN.
LIVE IN HARMONY WITH ONE ANOTHER.
DO NOT BE PROUD, BUT BE WILLING TO
ASSOCIATE WITH PEOPLE OF LOW POSITION.
DO NOT BE CONCEITED.
DO NOT REPAY ANYONE EVIL FOR EVIL.
BE CAREFUL TO DO WHAT IS RIGHT IN THE EYES
OF EVERYBODY.
IF IT IS POSSIBLE, AS FAR AS IT DEPENDS ON YOU,
LIVE AT PEACE WITH EVERYONE.

DO NOT TAKE REVENGE, MY FRIENDS, BUT LEAVE
ROOM FOR GOD'S WRATH, FOR IT IS WRITTEN:
"IT IS MINE TO AVENGE; I WILL REPAY," SAYS THE LORD.
ON THE CONTRARY:
"IF YOUR ENEMY IS HUNGRY, FEED HIM;
IF HE IS THIRSTY, GIVE HIM SOMETHING TO DRINK.
IN DOING THIS, YOU WILL HEAP BURNING COALS
ON HIS HEAD."
DO NOT BE OVERCOME BY EVIL, BUT OVERCOME
EVIL WITH GOOD.

MEDITATE AND ASK JEHOVAH TO OPEN YOUR EYES

THE FRUITS OF THE SPIRIT IS THE STRONG GLUE THAT SHOULD BIND THE ELECT FAMILY,

JEWS AND GENTILES.
GALATIANS 5:22-26

BUT THE FRUIT OF THE SPIRIT IS;

LOVE, JOY, PEACE, PATIENCE, KINDNESS,
GOODNESS, FAITHFULNESS, GENTLENESS AND
SELF-CONTROL.

AGAINST SUCH THINGS THERE IS NO LAW.

THOSE WHO BELONG TO CHRIST JESUS HAVE
CRUCIFIED THE SINFUL NATURE
WITH ITS PASSIONS AND DESIRES.

SINCE WE LIVE BY THE SPIRIT,

LET US KEEP IN STEP WITH THE SPIRIT.

LET US NOT BECOME CONCEITED,
PROVOKING AND ENVYING EACH OTHER.

MEDITATE AND ASK JEHOVAH TO OPEN YOUR EYES

WE MUST PRAISE JESUS ALL DAY

PSALM 150

PRAISE THE LORD.

PRAISE GOD IN HIS SANCTUARY;

PRAISE HIM IN HIS MIGHTY HEAVENS.

PRAISE HIM FOR HIS ACTS OF POWER;

PRAISE HIM FOR HIS SURPASSING GREATNESS.

PRAISE HIM WITH THE SOUNDING OF THE
TRUMPET,

PRAISE HIM WITH THE HARP AND LYRE,

PRAISE HIM WITH TAMBOURINE AND DANCING,

PRAISE HIM WITH THE STRINGS AND FLUTE,

PRAISE HIM WITH THE CLASH OF CYMBALS,

PRAISE HIM WITH RESOUNDING CYMBALS.

LET EVERYTHING THAT HAS BREATH PRAISE THE LORD.
PRAISE THE LORD.

MEDITATE AND ASK JEHOVAH TO OPEN YOUR EYES

CHURCH IS GOOD BUT, NOW IS CRUNCH TIME,

STICK YOUR HEAD IN A BIBLE

TO KNOW IF THE PREACHER IS NOT TELLING YOU
THE TRUTH.
BE A BEREAN(ACTS 17:11)

PSALM 1

BLESSED IS THE MAN

WHO DOES NOT WALK IN THE COUNSEL OF THE
WICKED

OR STAND IN THE WAY OF SINNERS

OR SIT IN THE SEAT OF MOCKERS.

BUT HIS DELIGHT IS IN THE LAW OF THE LORD,

AND ON HIS LAW HE MEDITATES DAY AND NIGHT.

HE IS LIKE A TREE PLANTED BY STREAMS OF WATER,

WHICH YIELDS ITS FRUIT IN SEASON

AND WHOSE LEAF DOES NOT WITHER.

WHATEVER HE DOES PROSPERS.

MEDITATE AND ASK JEHOVAH TO OPEN YOUR EYES

WORSHIP TO YOUR HEARTS DESIRE
FOR JEHOVAH

KING DAVID DANCE FOR GOD THEN, YOU DO TOO.

2 SAMUEL 6:14-15

WEARING A LINEN EPHOD,

DAVID WAS DANCING BEFORE THE LORD WITH ALL

HIS MIGHT,

WHILE HE AND ALL ISRAEL WERE BRINGING UP
THE ARK

OF THE

LORD WITH SHOUTS AND THE SOUND OF

TRUMPETS.

WE ALL CLAIM WE ARE WAITING FOR JESUS TO RETURN.

HOW IS JESUS GOING TO RETURN WITH THE WORLD AND THE BODY OF CHRIST IN TOTAL CHAOS. EVERY BODY IS DOING THEIR OWN THING CLAIMING THEY ARE FOLLOWING THE BIBLE. THEY ARE ALL PUFFING UP THEIR OWN CHEST, BECAUSE THEY ARE NOT LOOKING AT THE WHOLE BODY OF CHRIST AS ONE UNITED BODY. THE REASON ELIJAH AND JOHN THE BAPTIST CAME WAS TO CREATE ORDER. PRESENTLY THERE IS NO ORDER, THEREFORE JESUS IS NOT COMING SOON. ANYBODY WHO TELLS YOU ANYTHING DIFFERENT IS A LIAR.

1 CORINTHIANS 12:14-27

EVEN SO THE BODY IS NOT MADE UP OF ONE PART BUT OF MANY.
15 NOW IF THE FOOT SHOULD SAY,
"BECAUSE I AM NOT A HAND, I DO NOT BELONG TO THE BODY,"
(THE JEWS CAN NOT SAY WE DO NOT NEED THE GENTILES AND THE GENTILES CAN NOT SAY I DO NOT NEED THE JEWS)
IT WOULD NOT FOR THAT REASON STOP BEING PART OF THE BODY.
AND IF THE EAR SHOULD SAY, "BECAUSE I AM NOT AN EYE, I DO NOT BELONG TO THE BODY," IT WOULD NOT FOR THAT REASON STOP BEING PART OF THE BODY.

(THE JEWS CAN NOT SAY WE DO NOT NEED THE
GENTILES AND THE GENTILES CAN NOT SAY I DO
NOT NEED THE JEWS)
IF THE WHOLE BODY WERE AN EYE, WHERE WOULD
THE SENSE OF HEARING BE? IF THE WHOLE BODY
WERE AN EAR, WHERE WOULD THE SENSE OF SMELL
BE?
BUT IN FACT:
GOD HAS PLACED THE PARTS IN THE BODY, EVERY
ONE OF THEM, JUST AS HE WANTED THEM TO BE.
IF THEY WERE ALL ONE PART, WHERE WOULD THE
BODY BE?
AS IT IS, THERE ARE MANY PARTS, BUT ONE BODY.
THE EYE CANNOT SAY TO THE HAND, "I DON'T NEED
YOU!" AND THE HEAD CANNOT SAY TO THE FEET, "I
DON'T NEED YOU!"
(THE JEWS CAN NOT SAY WE DO NOT NEED THE
GENTILES AND THE GENTILES CAN NOT SAY I DO
NOT NEED THE JEWS)
ON THE CONTRARY, THOSE PARTS OF THE BODY
THAT SEEM TO BE WEAKER ARE INDISPENSABLE,
(JEWS, SMALL CHURCHES, THE POOR, PRISONERS,
ORPHAN AND WIDOWED)
AND THE PARTS THAT WE THINK ARE LESS
HONORABLE WE TREAT WITH SPECIAL HONOR. AND
THE PARTS THAT ARE UNPRESENTABLE ARE TREATED
WITH SPECIAL MODESTY,
(TREAT THESE WITH HONOR; JEWS, SMALL
CHURCHES, THE POOR, PRISONERS, ORPHAN AND
WIDOWED)
WHILE OUR PRESENTABLE PARTS NEED NO SPECIAL
TREATMENT. BUT GOD HAS PUT THE BODY
TOGETHER, GIVING GREATER HONOR TO THE
PARTS THAT LACKED IT,(JEWS, SMALL CHURCHES,
THE POOR, PRISONERS, ORPHAN AND WIDOWED)
SO THAT THERE SHOULD BE NO DIVISION IN THE
BODY, BUT THAT ITS PARTS SHOULD HAVE EQUAL
CONCERN FOR EACH OTHER.(BIG CHURCHES

MUST HAVE MORE CONCERN FOR; JEWS, SMALL
CHURCHES, THE POOR, PRISONERS, ORPHAN AND
WIDOWED)
IF ONE PART SUFFERS, EVERY PART SUFFERS WITH
IT; IF ONE PART IS HONORED, EVERY PART REJOICES
WITH IT.
(IN GOD'S EYES EVEN THOUGH LARGE CHURCHES
ARE DOING BETTER, IF THE JEWS, THE SMALL
CHURCHES, THE POOR, PRISONERS, ORPHAN AND
WIDOWED SUFFER, IN GOD'S EYES ALL IS SUFFERING,
THE WHOLE BODY OF CHRIST. IF BIG CHURCHES
ARE HAPPY, JEWS, THE SMALL CHURCHES, THE POOR,
PRISONERS, ORPHAN AND WIDOWED SHOULD
ALSO BE HAPPY.)

NOW YOU ARE THE BODY OF CHRIST, AND EACH
ONE OF YOU IS A PART OF IT.

MEDITATE AND ASK JEHOVAH TO OPEN YOUR EYES

PASTORS AND RABBIS OF THIS WORLD, ARE YOU NEIGHBORS TO EACH OTHER?

DOES LOVE EVEN MATTER TO ANY OF YOU?

LETS SEE NOW. JEHOVAH IS LOVE AND, YOU PASTORS AND RABBIS SUPPOSE TO BE CREATED IN THE IMAGE OF GOD. THEREFORE, YOU SHOULD BE LOVE ALSO. BUT, ARE YOU? BASED ON YOUR PRESENT BEHAVIOR, YOU HAVE SHOWN YOURSELVES TO BE VERY FAR FROM JEHOVAHS EXPECTATIONS OF YOU. YOU GUYS ARE A BUNCH OF BLIND GUIDES. I AM VERY SORRY FOR ANY HUMAN BEING WHO FOLLOW YOU.

LUKE 10:25, 29-37

ON ONE OCCASION AN EXPERT IN THE LAW(SOME OF TODAYS PASTORS AND RABBIS) STOOD UP TO TEST JESUS.
HE ASKED JESUS, "AND WHO IS MY NEIGHBOR?"

IN REPLY JESUS SAID: "A MAN WAS GOING DOWN FROM JERUSALEM TO JERICHO, WHEN HE FELL INTO THE HANDS OF ROBBERS. THEY STRIPPED HIM OF HIS CLOTHES, BEAT HIM AND WENT AWAY, LEAVING HIM HALF DEAD. A PRIEST(PASTOR) HAPPENED TO BE GOING DOWN THE SAME ROAD, AND WHEN HE SAW THE MAN, HE PASSED BY ON THE OTHER SIDE. SO TOO, A LEVITE(RABBI), WHEN HE CAME TO THE

PLACE AND SAW HIM, PASSED BY ON THE OTHER SIDE.

BUT A SAMARITAN(A NON-ELECT PERSON), AS HE TRAVELED, CAME WHERE THE MAN WAS; AND WHEN HE SAW HIM, HE TOOK PITY ON HIM. HE WENT TO HIM AND BANDAGED HIS WOUNDS, POURING ON OIL AND WINE. THEN HE PUT THE MAN ON HIS OWN DONKEY, TOOK HIM TO AN INN AND TOOK CARE OF HIM.

THE NEXT DAY HE TOOK OUT TWO SILVER COINS AND GAVE THEM TO THE INNKEEPER. 'LOOK AFTER HIM,' HE SAID, 'AND WHEN I RETURN, I WILL REIMBURSE YOU FOR ANY EXTRA EXPENSE YOU MAY HAVE.'

"WHICH OF THESE THREE DO YOU THINK WAS A NEIGHBOR TO THE MAN WHO FELL INTO THE HANDS OF ROBBERS?"
THE EXPERT IN THE LAW REPLIED, "THE ONE WHO HAD MERCY ON HIM."

JESUS TOLD HIM, "GO AND DO LIKEWISE."

MEDITATE AND ASK JEHOVAH TO OPEN YOUR EYES

I WILL BLESS THOSE WHO BLESS YOU

GENESIS 12:3
TO THE JEWS, JEHOVAH SAYS,
"I WILL BLESS THOSE WHO BLESS YOU,
AND WHOEVER CURSES YOU I WILL CURSE;
AND
ALL PEOPLES ON EARTH
WILL BE BLESSED THROUGH YOU."

TWO JEWISH ORGANIZATIONS THE
ELECTED BODY OF JESUS CHRIST

MUST HELP TODAY ARE:

STOP JEWISH ABORTIONS IN ISRAEL

BE'AD CHAIM ISRAEL

P.O. BOX 7974,

JERUSALEM 91078, ISRAEL

972-2-6242516
=
BRING LONG LOST JEWS BACK TO ISRAEL

ON WINGS OF EAGLES

INTERNATIONAL FELLOWSHIP

OF

CHRISTIAN AND JEWS

P.O. BOX 96105

WASHINGTON, D.C. 20090

312-641-7200
MAY JEHOVAH SCRIPTURES BE FULFILLED AS
WRITTEN, HALLELUJAH

MEDITATE AND ASK JEHOVAH TO OPEN YOUR EYES

I ASK YOU, DO WE FOLLOW MANS WORD ABOUT THE LAW OR JESUS?

MATTHEW 5:17-20
THE FULFILLMENT OF THE LAW

JESUS SAID,

"DO NOT THINK THAT I HAVE COME TO ABOLISH
THE LAW OR THE PROPHETS;

I HAVE NOT COME TO ABOLISH THEM BUT TO
FULFILL THEM.

I TELL YOU THE TRUTH, UNTIL HEAVEN AND
EARTH DISAPPEAR,

NOT THE SMALLEST LETTER, NOT THE LEAST
STROKE OF A PEN,

WILL BY ANY MEANS DISAPPEAR FROM THE LAW
UNTIL EVERYTHING IS ACCOMPLISHED.

ANYONE WHO BREAKS ONE OF THE LEAST OF
THESE COMMANDMENTS

AND

TEACHES OTHERS TO DO THE SAME

WILL BE CALLED LEAST IN THE KINGDOM OF
HEAVEN,

BUT WHOEVER PRACTICES AND TEACHES THESE
COMMANDS

WILL BE CALLED GREAT IN THE KINGDOM OF
HEAVEN.

FOR I TELL YOU THAT UNLESS YOUR
RIGHTEOUSNESS

SURPASSES THAT OF THE PHARISEES AND THE
TEACHERS OF THE LAW,

YOU WILL CERTAINLY NOT ENTER THE KINGDOM
OF HEAVEN.

MEDITATE AND ASK JEHOVAH TO OPEN YOUR EYES

THE TEN COMMANDMENTS

JEHOVAH'S LAWS WILL BE PRESENT IN OUR LIVES FOREVER

MATTHEW 19:17

"WHY DO YOU ASK ME ABOUT WHAT IS GOOD?" JESUS REPLIED.
"THERE IS ONLY ONE WHO IS GOOD. IF YOU WANT TO ENTER LIFE, OBEY THE COMMANDMENTS."

IF YOU HAVE DONE ANY OF THE FOLLOWING YOU ARE A SINNER.

1. YOU SHALL HAVE NO OTHER GODS BEFORE ME.

2. YOU SHALL NOT MAKE FOR YOURSELF AN IDOL IN THE FORM OF ANYTHING IN HEAVEN ABOVE OR ON THE EARTH BENEATH OR IN THE WATERS BELOW. YOU SHALL NOT BOW DOWN TO THEM OR WORSHIP THEM.

3. YOU SHALL NOT MISUSE THE NAME OF THE LORD YOUR GOD.

4. REMEMBER THE SABBATH DAY BY KEEPING IT HOLY. SIX DAYS YOU SHALL LABOR AND DO ALL YOUR WORK, BUT THE SEVENTH DAY IS A SABBATH TO THE LORD YOUR GOD.

5. HONOR YOUR FATHER AND YOUR MOTHER.

6. YOU SHALL NOT MURDER.

7. YOU SHALL NOT COMMIT ADULTERY.

8. YOU SHALL NOT STEAL.

9. YOU SHALL NOT GIVE FALSE TESTIMONY (LIAR)
AGAINST YOUR NEIGHBOR.

YOU SHALL NOT COVET YOUR NEIGHBOR'S
HOUSE. YOU SHALL NOT COVET (DESIRE) YOUR
NEIGHBOR'S WIFE, OR HIS MANSERVANT OR
MAIDSERVANT, HIS OX OR DONKEY, OR ANYTHING
THAT BELONGS TO YOUR NEIGHBOR.

PRAY TO JESUS CHRIST INCESSANTLY AND HE WILL
PROVIDE FOR YOU

IT IS EASIER FOR HEAVEN AND EARTH TO
DISAPPEAR THAN FOR THE LEAST STROKE OF A PEN
TO DROP OUT OF THE LAW.(LUKE 16:17)

MEDITATE AND ASK JEHOVAH TO OPEN YOUR EYES

THE WISE AND FOOLISH BUILDERS

LUKE 6:46-49

LORD JESUS SAID,

"WHY DO YOU CALL ME, 'LORD, LORD,' AND DO NOT DO WHAT I SAY? I WILL SHOW YOU WHAT HE IS LIKE WHO

COMES TO ME AND HEARS MY WORDS AND PUTS THEM INTO PRACTICE. HE IS LIKE A MAN BUILDING A HOUSE, WHO

DUG DOWN DEEP AND LAID THE FOUNDATION ON ROCK. WHEN A FLOOD CAME, THE TORRENT STRUCK THAT HOUSE BUT

COULD NOT SHAKE IT, BECAUSE IT WAS WELL BUILT. BUT THE ONE WHO HEARS MY WORDS AND DOES NOT PUT THEM

INTO PRACTICE IS LIKE A MAN WHO BUILT A HOUSE ON THE GROUND WITHOUT A FOUNDATION. THE MOMENT THE

TORRENT STRUCK THAT HOUSE, IT COLLAPSED AND ITS DESTRUCTION WAS COMPLETE."

MEDITATE AND ASK JEHOVAH TO OPEN YOUR EYES

JESUS IS GREATER THAN THE SABBATH

MATTHEW 12

1 AT THAT TIME JESUS (1)WENT THROUGH THE GRAINFIELDS ON THE SABBATH. HIS DISCIPLES WERE HUNGRY(HUNGRY PEOPLE) AND BEGAN TO (2)PICK SOME HEADS OF GRAIN AND (3)EAT THEM.

2 WHEN THE PHARISEES SAW THIS, THEY SAID TO HIM, "LOOK! YOUR DISCIPLES ARE DOING WHAT IS UNLAWFUL ON THE SABBATH."

3 HE ANSWERED, "HAVEN'T YOU READ WHAT DAVID DID WHEN HE AND HIS COMPANIONS WERE HUNGRY?

4 HE (4)ENTERED THE HOUSE OF GOD, AND HE AND HIS COMPANIONS (5)ATE THE CONSECRATED BREAD(DAVID FED HUNGRY PEOPLE ON THE SABBATH. SOME PEOPLE ARE HUNGRY FOR FOOD. SOME PEOPLE ARE HUNGRY FOR THE WORD OF GOD.)—WHICH WAS NOT LAWFUL FOR THEM TO DO, BUT ONLY FOR THE PRIESTS.

5 OR HAVEN'T YOU READ IN THE LAW THAT (6)THE PRIESTS ON SABBATH DUTY IN THE TEMPLE DESECRATE THE SABBATH AND YET ARE INNOCENT?

6 I TELL YOU THAT SOMETHING GREATER THAN THE TEMPLE IS HERE.

7 IF YOU HAD KNOWN WHAT THESE WORDS MEAN, 'I DESIRE MERCY(JESUS WANTS FORGIVENESS AND HELPING PEOPLE IN THE NAME OF JESUS CHRIST TO BE FIRST ON THE SABBATH), NOT SACRIFICE(JESUS DO

NOT WANT US TO PUT OUR PERSONAL SACRIFICES ABOVE FORGIVENESS AND HELPING OTHERS IN HIS NAME ON THE SABBATH),' YOU WOULD NOT HAVE CONDEMNED THE INNOCENT(BY US NOT HELPING FRIENDS, FAMILY AND STRANGERS IN JESUS NAME ON THE SABBATH, WE ARE DEPRIVING OURSELVES OPPORTUNITIES TO SHARE THE WORD ABOUT JESUS. HENCE, MANY PEOPLE WHO COULD BE SAVED WILL NOT BE SAVED, BECAUSE NO ONE WOULD HAVE PREACHED TO THEM).

8 FOR THE SON OF MAN IS LORD OF THE SABBATH(DOING WORK FOR JESUS IS ABOVE ANY AND ALL SABBATH RULES BUT, THE SABBATH SHOULD BE OBSERVED)."

9 GOING ON FROM THAT PLACE, (7)HE WENT INTO THEIR SYNAGOGUE,

10 AND A MAN WITH A SHRIVELED HAND WAS THERE. LOOKING FOR A REASON TO BRING CHARGES AGAINST JESUS, THEY ASKED HIM, "IS IT LAWFUL TO HEAL ON THE SABBATH?"

11 HE SAID TO THEM, "IF ANY OF YOU HAS A SHEEP AND IT FALLS INTO A PIT ON THE SABBATH(JESUS ACKNOWLEDGES THE SABBATH), WILL YOU NOT TAKE HOLD OF IT AND LIFT IT OUT?

12 HOW MUCH MORE VALUABLE IS A PERSON THAN A SHEEP! THEREFORE IT IS LAWFUL TO DO GOOD ON THE SABBATH."

13 THEN (8)HE SAID TO THE MAN, "STRETCH OUT YOUR HAND." SO HE STRETCHED IT OUT AND IT WAS COMPLETELY RESTORED, JUST AS SOUND AS THE OTHER.

MEDITATE AND ASK JEHOVAH TO OPEN YOUR EYES

THE SABBATH DAY

YOUR QUESTION TO ME:

YES, WE MUST CELEBRATE THE SABBATH DAY. JESUS
ASKED US TO DO SO.
WHEN DO WE CELEBRATE THE SABBATH DAY?

AS YOU ANSWER THE FOLLOWING QUESTIONS,

YOU WILL ARRIVE AT YOUR OWN ANSWER.

QUESTION ONE:

WHAT DOES THE BIBLE SAY
ABOUT THE FIRST SEVEN DAYS
AT THE START OF THE UNIVERSE?

QUESTION TWO:

DO YOU HAVE ENOUGH INFORMATION
TO KNOW WHEN THE SEVEN DAYS
STARTED OR ENDED?

QUESTION THREE:

FROM WHOM DID YOU GET YOUR INFORMATION,
ABOUT THE GOD YOU BELIEVE IN, JESUS CHRIST?

QUESTION FOUR:

HOW DO THEY CELEBRATE THE SABBATH DAY?

QUESTION FIVE:

WHY DO WE FOLLOW THE GIVERS OF THE GODLY
INFORMATION,
IN EVERY OTHER ASPECT BUT,
HOW THEY CELEBRATE THE SABBATH DAY,
WHICH IS ALSO ONE OF THE GREATEST
COMMANDMENTS?

QUESTION SIX:

SO, YOU TELL ME, WHEN IS THE SABBATH DAY
SUPPOSED TO BE CELEBRATED?

MEDITATE AND ASK JEHOVAH TO OPEN YOUR EYES

COMMUNION CAN BE TAKEN DAILY AND MULTIPLE TIMES DAILY,

BY ANYONE ANYWHERE. THERE IS NO LIMIT DAYS OR TIMES.

THE MORE YOU TAKE COMMUNION THE STRONGER YOU ARE
SPIRITUALLY AND PHYSICALLY: "DEMONS STAY AWAY"
BE SERIOUS ABOUT YOUR REPENTING:
(1 CORINTHIANS 11:29)
FOR THOSE WHO EAT AND DRINK WITHOUT DISCERNING THE BODY OF CHRIST
EAT AND DRINK JUDGMENT ON THEMSELVES.
LAST SUPPER PRAYER "EXPRESS YOUR LOVE FOR JESUS DAILY"
DON'T BE AFRAID, LOVE ALL AND HAVE MERCY ON OTHERS

1 CORINTHIANS 11:23-26

THE LORD JESUS, ON THE NIGHT HE WAS BETRAYED, TOOK BREAD AND WHEN HE HAD GIVEN THANKS, HE BROKE IT AND SAID, "THIS IS MY BODY, WHICH IS FOR YOU; DO THIS IN REMEMBRANCE OF ME."

IN THE SAME WAY, AFTER SUPPER HE TOOK THE CUP, SAYING, "THIS CUP IS THE NEW COVENANT IN MY BLOOD; DO THIS, WHENEVER YOU DRINK IT, IN REMEMBRANCE OF ME. FOR WHENEVER YOU EAT

THIS BREAD AND DRINK THIS CUP, YOU PROCLAIM
THE LORD'S DEATH UNTIL HE COMES.
MARK 14:22-25

WHILE THEY WERE EATING, JESUS TOOK BREAD,
GAVE THANKS AND BROKE IT, AND GAVE IT TO HIS
DISCIPLES, SAYING, "TAKE IT; THIS IS MY BODY."
THEN HE TOOK THE CUP, GAVE THANKS AND OFFERED
IT TO THEM, AND THEY ALL DRANK FROM IT.
THIS IS MY BLOOD OF THE COVENANT, WHICH IS
POURED OUT FOR MANY," HE SAID TO THEM. 25 "I
TELL YOU THE TRUTH, I WILL NOT DRINK AGAIN
OF THE FRUIT OF THE VINE UNTIL THAT DAY WHEN
I DRINK IT ANEW IN THE KINGDOM OF GOD."
JOHN 6:56

HE WHO EATS MY FLESH AND DRINKS MY BLOOD
ABIDES IN ME, AND I IN HIM.

MEDITATE AND ASK JEHOVAH TO OPEN YOUR EYES

ARE YOU A SHEEP OR A GOAT?

DO YOU KNOW JESUS HAS STARTED SEPARATING THE SHEEP FROM THE GOATS ALREADY? IT'S REALLY INCREDIBLE HOW HE DOES IT, DURING YOUR WORSHIP TIME IN CHURCH IS ONE WAY HE DOES IT. HAVE YOU EVER WONDERED, HOW AFTER A BEAUTIFUL WORSHIP SESSION IN CHURCH, SOME PEOPLE WOULD SAY, THE WORSHIP WAS NOT GOOD. TO TELL YOU THE TRUTH, MOST LIKELY THEY ARE IN THE PROCESS OF BEING KICKED OUT OF THE CHURCH BY JESUS. NOT EVERYONE THAT LEAVES CHURCH LEAVES ON THEIR OWN ACORD. WHEN YOU ARE NOT ENJOYING WORSHIP IN CHURCH ASK YOURSELF WHY NOT? SOMETIMES IT COULD BE THE CHURCH BUT, MOST OF THE TIMES IT'S YOU.

MATTHEW 25:31-46

"WHEN THE SON OF MAN COMES IN HIS GLORY, AND ALL THE ANGELS WITH HIM, HE WILL SIT ON HIS THRONE IN HEAVENLY GLORY. ALL THE NATIONS WILL BE GATHERED BEFORE HIM, AND HE WILL SEPARATE THE PEOPLE ONE FROM ANOTHER AS A SHEPHERD SEPARATES THE SHEEP FROM THE GOATS. HE WILL PUT THE SHEEP ON HIS RIGHT AND THE GOATS ON HIS LEFT.

"THEN THE KING WILL SAY TO THOSE ON HIS RIGHT, 'COME, YOU WHO ARE BLESSED BY MY FATHER; TAKE YOUR INHERITANCE, THE KINGDOM PREPARED FOR YOU SINCE THE CREATION OF THE WORLD. FOR I WAS HUNGRY AND YOU GAVE ME SOMETHING TO EAT, I WAS THIRSTY AND YOU GAVE ME SOMETHING

TO DRINK, I WAS A STRANGER AND YOU INVITED ME IN, I NEEDED CLOTHES AND YOU CLOTHED ME, I WAS SICK AND YOU LOOKED AFTER ME, I WAS IN PRISON AND YOU CAME TO VISIT ME.'

"THEN THE RIGHTEOUS WILL ANSWER HIM, 'LORD, WHEN DID WE SEE YOU HUNGRY AND FEED YOU, OR THIRSTY AND GIVE YOU SOMETHING TO DRINK? WHEN DID WE SEE YOU A STRANGER AND INVITE YOU IN, OR NEEDING CLOTHES AND CLOTHE YOU? WHEN DID WE SEE YOU SICK OR IN PRISON AND GO TO VISIT YOU?'

"THE KING WILL REPLY, 'I TELL YOU THE TRUTH, WHATEVER YOU DID FOR ONE OF THE LEAST OF THESE BROTHERS OF MINE, YOU DID FOR ME.'

"THEN HE WILL SAY TO THOSE ON HIS LEFT, 'DEPART FROM ME, YOU WHO ARE CURSED, INTO THE ETERNAL FIRE PREPARED FOR THE DEVIL AND HIS ANGELS. FOR I WAS HUNGRY AND YOU GAVE ME NOTHING TO EAT, I WAS THIRSTY AND YOU GAVE ME NOTHING TO DRINK, I WAS A STRANGER AND YOU DID NOT INVITE ME IN, I NEEDED CLOTHES AND YOU DID NOT CLOTHE ME, I WAS SICK AND IN PRISON AND YOU DID NOT LOOK AFTER ME.'

"THEY ALSO WILL ANSWER, 'LORD, WHEN DID WE SEE YOU HUNGRY OR THIRSTY OR A STRANGER OR NEEDING CLOTHES OR SICK OR IN PRISON, AND DID NOT HELP YOU?'

"HE WILL REPLY, 'I TELL YOU THE TRUTH, WHATEVER YOU DID NOT DO FOR ONE OF THE LEAST OF THESE, YOU DID NOT DO FOR ME.'
"THEN THEY WILL GO AWAY TO ETERNAL PUNISHMENT, BUT THE RIGHTEOUS TO ETERNAL LIFE."

MEDITATE AND ASK JEHOVAH TO OPEN YOUR EYES

THE BEATITUDES

MATTHEW 5:1-12

NOW WHEN JESUS SAW THE CROWDS,
HE WENT UP ON A MOUNTAINSIDE AND SAT
DOWN.

HIS DISCIPLES CAME TO HIM,
AND HE BEGAN TO TEACH THEM, SAYING:

"BLESSED ARE THE POOR IN SPIRIT,
FOR THEIRS IS THE KINGDOM OF HEAVEN.

BLESSED ARE THOSE WHO MOURN,
FOR THEY WILL BE COMFORTED.

BLESSED ARE THE MEEK,
FOR THEY WILL INHERIT THE EARTH.

BLESSED ARE THOSE WHO HUNGER AND THIRST
FOR RIGHTEOUSNESS,
FOR THEY WILL BE FILLED.

BLESSED ARE THE MERCIFUL,
FOR THEY WILL BE SHOWN MERCY.

BLESSED ARE THE PURE IN HEART,
FOR THEY WILL SEE GOD.

BLESSED ARE THE PEACEMAKERS,
FOR THEY WILL BE CALLED SONS OF GOD.

BLESSED ARE THOSE WHO ARE PERSECUTED
BECAUSE OF RIGHTEOUSNESS,
FOR THEIRS IS THE KINGDOM OF HEAVEN.
"BLESSED ARE YOU WHEN PEOPLE INSULT YOU,
PERSECUTE YOU AND FALSELY SAY ALL KINDS OF
EVIL AGAINST YOU
BECAUSE OF ME.

REJOICE AND BE GLAD,
BECAUSE GREAT IS YOUR REWARD IN HEAVEN,
FOR IN THE SAME WAY THEY PERSECUTED THE
PROPHETS WHO WERE BEFORE YOU.

MEDITATE AND ASK JEHOVAH TO OPEN YOUR EYES

JESUS WANTS TO HAVE A RELATIONSHIP WITH YOU, TO SAVE YOU, AND TO TALK WITH YOU.

MATTHEW 12:38-42

38 THEN SOME OF THE PHARISEES AND TEACHERS OF THE LAW SAID TO JESUS, "TEACHER, WE WANT TO SEE A SIGN FROM YOU."

39 HE ANSWERED, "A WICKED AND ADULTEROUS GENERATION ASKS FOR A SIGN! BUT NONE WILL BE GIVEN IT EXCEPT THE SIGN OF THE PROPHET JONAH.

40 FOR AS JONAH WAS THREE DAYS AND THREE NIGHTS IN THE BELLY OF A HUGE FISH(JONAH WAS DEAD FOR THREE DAYS), SO THE SON OF MAN WILL BE THREE DAYS AND THREE NIGHTS IN THE HEART OF THE EARTH(JESUS WAS DEAD FOR THREE DAYS. IF JESUS WAS NOT DEAD, HE COULD NOT BE RESURRECTED).

41 THE MEN OF NINEVEH WILL STAND UP AT THE JUDGMENT WITH THIS GENERATION AND CONDEMN IT; FOR THEY REPENTED AT THE PREACHING OF JONAH(JONAH CAME BACK FROM THE DEAD AND PREACHED TO THE PEOPLE OF NINEVEY AND THEY GOT SAVED), AND NOW SOMETHING GREATER THAN JONAH IS HERE(I

JESUS THE MESSIAH GREATER THAN JONAH IS HERE TO SAVE YOU).

42 THE QUEEN OF THE SOUTH WILL RISE AT THE JUDGMENT WITH THIS GENERATION AND CONDEMN IT; FOR SHE CAME FROM THE ENDS OF THE EARTH TO LISTEN TO SOLOMON'S WISDOM(AT THAT TIME SOLOMON WAS THE WISEST MAN EVER LIVED AND THE QUEEN WAS THE WISEST WOMAN EVER LIVED), AND NOW SOMETHING GREATER THAN SOLOMON IS HERE(I JESUS THE CREATOR OF HEAVEN AND EARTH IS WITH YOU TO TALK WITH YOU AND TO DEVELOP A RELATIONSHIP WITH YOU).

MEDITATE AND ASK JEHOVAH TO OPEN YOUR EYES

WHY IS IT SO HARD FOR BACKSLIDERS TO RETURN TO CHRIST

WHEN WE FIRST ACCEPT JESUS AS OUR LORD AND SAVIOR, WE ARE EXCITED SO WE TRUST, PRAY AND WORSHIP HIM A GREAT DEAL WHILE ATTENDING CHURCH. BUT AS TIME GOES ON AND OUR PROBLEMS SEEM FAR AWAY, WE MOVE AWAY FROM CHRIST, REMOVING OUR PROTECTION FROM EVIL SPIRITS. AS WE MOVE AWAY FROM CHRIST, THE EVIL SPIRIT WHICH WAS ON US PRIOR TO ACCEPTING CHRIST, WHO HAD LEFT US, RETURNS TO US AND REALIZES WE ARE MORE VULNERABLE TO EVIL SPIRITS THAN WE EVER WERE. HENCE, HE GOES AND BRINGS MORE EVIL SPIRITS TO LIVE IN US WITH HIM. THEN, OUR LIVES BEGINS TO GET MUCH WORST THAN IT EVER WAS IN THE PAST.

WANTS YOU ACCEPT JESUS AS YOUR LORD AND SAVIOR DO NOT LET HIM GO.

MATTHEW 12:43-45

43 "WHEN AN IMPURE SPIRIT COMES OUT OF A PERSON, IT GOES THROUGH ARID PLACES SEEKING REST AND DOES NOT FIND IT.
44 THEN IT SAYS, 'I WILL RETURN TO THE HOUSE I LEFT.' WHEN IT ARRIVES, IT FINDS THE HOUSE UNOCCUPIED, SWEPT CLEAN AND PUT IN ORDER.
45 THEN IT GOES AND TAKES WITH IT SEVEN OTHER SPIRITS MORE WICKED THAN ITSELF, AND

THEY GO IN AND LIVE THERE. AND THE FINAL CONDITION OF THAT PERSON IS WORSE THAN THE FIRST. THAT IS HOW IT WILL BE WITH THIS WICKED GENERATION."

MEDITATE AND ASK JEHOVAH TO OPEN YOUR EYES

PUSH

P-PRAY

U-UNTIL

S-SOMETHING

H-HAPPENS

MEDITATE AND ASK JEHOVAH TO OPEN YOUR EYES

OUR JOB IS TO COPY WHAT THE TWELVE DISCIPLES DID.

WE HAVE TO TESTIFY WHO JESUS IS,

AND WHY HE CAME.

THAT IS THE GOOD NEWS.

"THE FATHER HAS SENT HIS SON TO BE THE
SAVIOR OF THE WORLD."
1 JOHN 4:14-16

AND WE HAVE SEEN AND TESTIFY
THAT THE FATHER HAS SENT HIS SON TO BE THE
SAVIOR OF THE WORLD.
IF ANYONE ACKNOWLEDGES THAT JESUS IS THE
SON OF GOD,
GOD LIVES IN HIM
AND HE IN GOD.
AND SO WE KNOW
AND
RELY ON THE LOVE GOD HAS FOR US.
GOD IS LOVE.
WHOEVER LIVES IN LOVE LIVES IN GOD,
AND
GOD IN HIM.

JOHN 8:31

THEN JESUS SAID TO THOSE JEWS WHO BELIEVED HIM,
"IF YOU ABIDE IN MY WORD, YOU ARE MY DISCIPLES INDEED.

MEDITATE AND ASK JEHOVAH TO OPEN YOUR EYES

MY HEALING PRAYER FOR YOU IS:

MAY JEHOVAH FORGIVE YOU/ME OF YOUR/MY
SINS
IN JESUS' NAME

MAY JESUS BLOW HIS BREATH OF LIFE
INTO YOUR/MY NOSTRILS.

MAY JESUS' BLOOD, WHICH IS JEHOVAH'S BLOOD,
RUN THROUGHOUT YOUR/MY VEINS.

MAY JESUS COMPASSION, LOVE AND MERCY
FALL ON YOU/ME.

MAY JESUS' FLESH BE YOUR/MY FLESH
AND MAY YOU/I BE HEALED OF ALL OF
YOUR/MY PHYSICAL OR MENTAL OR FAMILY ISSUES
IN YOUR/MY LIFE TODAY AND FOREVER MORE.

I ASK JEHOVAH IN JESUS'
PRECIOUS NAME

HALLELUJAH HALLELUJAH HALLELUJAH

AMEN & AMEN & AMEN

READ THIS PRAYER OVER AND OVER AGAIN

MEDITATE AND ASK JEHOVAH TO OPEN YOUR EYES

ACCORDING TO MY FAITH

IN MY LORD & SAVIOR JESUS CHRIST

BE

IT

DONE

ON

TO

ME

MEDITATE AND ASK JEHOVAH TO OPEN YOUR EYES

JEHOVAH HATES ARROGANCE

DUE TO YOUR ARROGANCE PASTORS, CARTHOLIC PRIEST & RABBIS,

YOU ALSO WILL BE REJECTED

PROVERBS 8:13

TO FEAR THE LORD IS TO HATE EVIL;
I HATE PRIDE AND ARROGANCE,
EVIL BEHAVIOR AND PERVERSE SPEECH.

ISAIAH 13:11

I WILL PUNISH THE WORLD FOR ITS EVIL,
THE WICKED FOR THEIR SINS.
I WILL PUT AN END TO THE ARROGANCE OF THE
HAUGHTY
AND
WILL HUMBLE THE PRIDE OF THE RUTHLESS.

1 SAMUEL 15:23

FOR REBELLION IS LIKE THE SIN OF DIVINATION,
AND
ARROGANCE LIKE THE EVIL OF IDOLATRY.
BECAUSE YOU HAVE REJECTED THE WORD OF THE
LORD,
HE HAS REJECTED YOU AS KING."

MEDITATE AND ASK JEHOVAH TO OPEN YOUR EYES

FASTING THAT JEHOVAH WANTS

LUKE 5:33-39

34 JESUS ANSWERED,
"CAN YOU MAKE THE GUESTS OF THE
BRIDEGROOM FAST WHILE HE IS WITH THEM?
35 BUT THE TIME WILL COME WHEN THE
BRIDEGROOM WILL BE TAKEN FROM THEM;
IN THOSE DAYS THEY WILL FAST."

ISAIAH 58:6-11

THE MESSAGE (MSG)

6-9"THIS IS THE KIND OF FAST DAY I'M AFTER:
TO BREAK THE CHAINS OF INJUSTICE,
GET RID OF EXPLOITATION IN THE WORKPLACE,
FREE THE OPPRESSED,
CANCEL DEBTS.
WHAT I'M INTERESTED IN SEEING YOU DO IS:
SHARING YOUR FOOD WITH THE HUNGRY,
INVITING THE HOMELESS POOR INTO YOUR
HOMES,
PUTTING CLOTHES ON THE SHIVERING ILL-CLAD,
BEING AVAILABLE TO YOUR OWN FAMILIES.
DO THIS AND THE LIGHTS WILL TURN ON,
AND YOUR LIVES WILL TURN AROUND AT ONCE.
YOUR RIGHTEOUSNESS WILL PAVE YOUR WAY.
THE GOD OF GLORY WILL SECURE YOUR PASSAGE.
THEN WHEN YOU PRAY, GOD WILL ANSWER.

YOU'LL CALL OUT FOR HELP AND I'LL SAY, 'HERE I
AM.'

A FULL LIFE IN THE EMPTIEST OF PLACES

9-12"IF YOU GET RID OF UNFAIR PRACTICES,
QUIT BLAMING VICTIMS,
QUIT GOSSIPING ABOUT OTHER PEOPLE'S SINS,
IF YOU ARE GENEROUS WITH THE HUNGRY
AND START GIVING YOURSELVES TO THE
DOWN-AND-OUT,
YOUR LIVES WILL BEGIN TO GLOW IN THE
DARKNESS,
YOUR SHADOWED LIVES WILL BE BATHED IN
SUNLIGHT.
I WILL ALWAYS SHOW YOU WHERE TO GO.
I'LL GIVE YOU A FULL LIFE IN THE EMPTIEST OF
PLACES—
FIRM MUSCLES, STRONG BONES.
YOU'LL BE LIKE A WELL-WATERED GARDEN,
A GURGLING SPRING THAT NEVER RUNS DRY.

MEDITATE AND ASK JEHOVAH TO OPEN YOUR EYES

GOD LOVES THE HUMBLE

PAGE ONE
- EXODUS 10:3*
  SO MOSES AND AARON WENT TO PHARAOH AND SAID TO HIM, "THIS IS WHAT THE LORD, THE GOD OF THE HEBREWS, SAYS: 'HOW LONG WILL YOU REFUSE TO HUMBLE YOURSELF BEFORE ME? LET MY PEOPLE GO, SO THAT THEY MAY WORSHIP ME.
- NUMBERS 12:3*
  (NOW MOSES WAS A VERY HUMBLE MAN, MORE HUMBLE THAN ANYONE ELSE ON THE FACE OF THE EARTH.)
- DEUTERONOMY 8:2*
  REMEMBER HOW THE LORD YOUR GOD LED YOU ALL THE WAY IN THE DESERT THESE FORTY YEARS, TO HUMBLE YOU AND TO TEST YOU IN ORDER TO KNOW WHAT WAS IN YOUR HEART, WHETHER OR NOT YOU WOULD KEEP HIS COMMANDS.
- DEUTERONOMY 8:3*
  HE HUMBLED YOU, CAUSING YOU TO HUNGER AND THEN FEEDING YOU WITH MANNA, WHICH NEITHER YOU NOR YOUR FATHERS HAD KNOWN, TO TEACH YOU THAT MAN DOES NOT LIVE ON BREAD ALONE BUT

ON EVERY WORD THAT COMES FROM THE MOUTH OF THE LORD.

- 1 SAMUEL 2:7*
  THE LORD SENDS POVERTY AND WEALTH; HE HUMBLES AND HE EXALTS.
- 2 SAMUEL 22:28*
  YOU SAVE THE HUMBLE, BUT YOUR EYES ARE ON THE HAUGHTY TO BRING THEM LOW.
- 1 KINGS 11:39*
  I WILL HUMBLE DAVID'S DESCENDANTS BECAUSE OF THIS, BUT NOT FOREVER.'"
- 2 CHRONICLES 7:14*
  IF MY PEOPLE, WHO ARE CALLED BY MY NAME, WILL HUMBLE THEMSELVES AND PRAY AND SEEK MY FACE AND TURN FROM THEIR WICKED WAYS, THEN WILL I HEAR FROM HEAVEN AND WILL FORGIVE THEIR SIN AND WILL HEAL THEIR LAND.

MEDITATE AND ASK JEHOVAH TO OPEN YOUR EYES

GOD LOVES THE HUMBLE

PAGE TWO

- 2 CHRONICLES 12:7*
  WHEN THE LORD SAW THAT THEY HUMBLED
  THEMSELVES, THIS WORD OF THE LORD CAME
  TO SHEMAIAH: "SINCE THEY HAVE HUMBLED
  THEMSELVES, I WILL NOT DESTROY THEM
  BUT WILL SOON GIVE THEM DELIVERANCE.
  MY WRATH WILL NOT BE POURED OUT ON
  JERUSALEM THROUGH SHISHAK.
- 2 CHRONICLES 28:19*
  THE LORD HAD HUMBLED JUDAH(AMERICA)
  BECAUSE OF AHAZ KING OF ISRAEL, FOR
  HE HAD PROMOTED WICKEDNESS IN
  JUDAH(AMERICA) AND HAD BEEN MOST
  UNFAITHFUL TO THE LORD.
- 2 CHRONICLES 34:27*
  BECAUSE YOUR HEART WAS RESPONSIVE AND
  YOU HUMBLED YOURSELF BEFORE GOD WHEN
  YOU HEARD WHAT HE SPOKE AGAINST THIS
  PLACE AND ITS PEOPLE, AND BECAUSE YOU
  HUMBLED YOURSELF BEFORE ME AND TORE
  YOUR ROBES AND WEPT IN MY PRESENCE, I
  HAVE HEARD YOU, DECLARES THE LORD.

- PSALM 18:27*
  YOU SAVE THE HUMBLE BUT BRING LOW
  THOSE WHOSE EYES ARE HAUGHTY.
- PSALM 25:9*
  HE GUIDES THE HUMBLE IN WHAT IS RIGHT
  AND TEACHES THEM HIS WAY.
- PSALM 107:39*
  THEN THEIR(ISRAEL) NUMBERS DECREASED,
  AND THEY WERE HUMBLED BY OPPRESSION,
  CALAMITY AND SORROW;
- PSALM 147:6*
  THE LORD SUSTAINS THE HUMBLE BUT CASTS
  THE WICKED TO THE GROUND.
- PSALM 149:4*
  FOR THE LORD TAKES DELIGHT IN HIS PEOPLE;
  HE CROWNS THE HUMBLE WITH SALVATION.

MEDITATE AND ASK JEHOVAH TO OPEN YOUR EYES

GOD LOVES THE HUMBLE

PAGE THREE

- ISAIAH 2:11*
  THE EYES OF THE ARROGANT MAN WILL BE
  HUMBLED AND THE PRIDE OF MEN BROUGHT
  LOW; THE LORD ALONE WILL BE EXALTED IN
  THAT DAY.
- ISAIAH 2:12*
  THE LORD ALMIGHTY HAS A DAY IN STORE FOR
  ALL THE PROUD AND LOFTY, FOR ALL THAT IS
  EXALTED (AND THEY WILL BE HUMBLED),
- ISAIAH 2:17*
  THE ARROGANCE OF MAN WILL BE BROUGHT
  LOW AND THE PRIDE OF MEN HUMBLED; THE
  LORD ALONE WILL BE EXALTED IN THAT DAY,
- ISAIAH 5:15*
  SO MAN WILL BE BROUGHT LOW AND
  MANKIND HUMBLED, THE EYES OF THE
  ARROGANT HUMBLED.
- ISAIAH 13:11*
  I WILL PUNISH THE WORLD FOR ITS EVIL, THE
  WICKED FOR THEIR SINS. I WILL PUT AN END
  TO THE ARROGANCE OF THE HAUGHTY AND
  WILL HUMBLE THE PRIDE OF THE RUTHLESS.

- ISAIAH 23:9*
  THE LORD ALMIGHTY PLANNED IT, TO BRING
  LOW THE PRIDE OF ALL GLORY AND TO
  HUMBLE ALL WHO ARE RENOWNED ON THE
  EARTH.
- ISAIAH 26:5*
  HE HUMBLES THOSE WHO DWELL ON HIGH,
  HE LAYS THE LOFTY CITY LOW(NY-9/11); HE
  LEVELS IT TO THE GROUND AND CASTS IT
  DOWN TO THE DUST.
- ISAIAH 29:19*
  ONCE MORE THE HUMBLE WILL REJOICE IN
  THE LORD; THE NEEDY WILL REJOICE IN THE
  HOLY ONE OF ISRAEL.

MEDITATE AND ASK JEHOVAH TO OPEN YOUR EYES

GOD LOVES THE HUMBLE

PAGE FOUR

- ISAIAH 66:2*
  HAS NOT MY HAND MADE ALL THESE THINGS,
  AND SO THEY CAME INTO BEING?" DECLARES
  THE LORD. "THIS IS THE ONE I ESTEEM: HE
  WHO IS HUMBLE AND CONTRITE IN SPIRIT,
  AND TREMBLES AT MY WORD.
- DANIEL 4:37*
  NOW I, NEBUCHADNEZZAR, PRAISE AND EXALT
  AND GLORIFY THE KING OF HEAVEN, BECAUSE
  EVERYTHING HE DOES IS RIGHT AND ALL HIS
  WAYS ARE JUST. AND THOSE WHO WALK IN
  PRIDE HE IS ABLE TO HUMBLE.
- DANIEL 10:12*
  THEN HE CONTINUED, "DO NOT BE AFRAID,
  DANIEL. SINCE THE FIRST DAY THAT YOU SET
  YOUR MIND TO GAIN UNDERSTANDING AND
  TO HUMBLE YOURSELF BEFORE YOUR GOD,
  YOUR WORDS WERE HEARD, AND I HAVE
  COME IN RESPONSE TO THEM.
- ZEPHANIAH 3:12*
  BUT I WILL LEAVE WITHIN YOU THE MEEK
  AND HUMBLE, WHO TRUST IN THE NAME OF
  THE LORD.

- MATTHEW 11:29*
  TAKE MY YOKE UPON YOU AND LEARN FROM ME, FOR I AM GENTLE AND HUMBLE IN HEART, AND YOU WILL FIND REST FOR YOUR SOULS.
- MATTHEW 18:4*
  THEREFORE, WHOEVER HUMBLES HIMSELF LIKE THIS CHILD IS THE GREATEST IN THE KINGDOM OF HEAVEN.
- MATTHEW 23:12*
  FOR WHOEVER EXALTS HIMSELF WILL BE HUMBLED, AND WHOEVER HUMBLES HIMSELF WILL BE EXALTED.
- LUKE 1:52*
  HE HAS BROUGHT DOWN RULERS FROM THEIR THRONES BUT HAS LIFTED UP THE HUMBLE.
- LUKE 14:11*
  FOR EVERYONE WHO EXALTS HIMSELF WILL BE HUMBLED, AND HE WHO HUMBLES HIMSELF WILL BE EXALTED."

MEDITATE AND ASK JEHOVAH TO OPEN YOUR EYES

GOD LOVES THE HUMBLE

PAGE FIVE

- LUKE 18:14*
  "I TELL YOU THAT THIS MAN, RATHER THAN THE OTHER, WENT HOME JUSTIFIED BEFORE GOD. FOR EVERYONE WHO EXALTS HIMSELF WILL BE HUMBLED, AND HE WHO HUMBLES HIMSELF WILL BE EXALTED."
- EPHESIANS 4:2*
  BE COMPLETELY HUMBLE AND GENTLE; BE PATIENT, BEARING WITH ONE ANOTHER IN LOVE.
- PHILIPPIANS 2:8*
  AND BEING FOUND IN APPEARANCE AS A MAN, HE HUMBLED HIMSELF AND BECAME OBEDIENT TO DEATH— EVEN DEATH ON A CROSS!
- JAMES 1:9*
  THE BROTHER IN HUMBLE CIRCUMSTANCES OUGHT TO TAKE PRIDE IN HIS HIGH POSITION.
- JAMES 4:6*
  BUT HE GIVES US MORE GRACE. THAT IS WHY SCRIPTURE SAYS: "GOD OPPOSES THE PROUD BUT GIVES GRACE TO THE HUMBLE."

- JAMES 4:10*
  HUMBLE YOURSELVES BEFORE THE LORD, AND HE WILL LIFT YOU UP.
- 1 PETER 3:8*
  FINALLY, ALL OF YOU, LIVE IN HARMONY WITH ONE ANOTHER; BE SYMPATHETIC, LOVE AS BROTHERS, BE COMPASSIONATE AND HUMBLE.
- 1 PETER 5:5*
  YOUNG MEN, IN THE SAME WAY BE SUBMISSIVE TO THOSE WHO ARE OLDER. ALL OF YOU, CLOTHE YOURSELVES WITH HUMILITY TOWARD ONE ANOTHER, BECAUSE, "GOD OPPOSES THE PROUD BUT GIVES GRACE TO THE HUMBLE."
- 1 PETER 5:6*
  HUMBLE YOURSELVES, THEREFORE, UNDER GOD'S MIGHTY HAND, THAT HE MAY LIFT YOU UP IN DUE TIME.

MEDITATE AND ASK JEHOVAH TO OPEN YOUR EYES

GOD LOVES THE HUMBLE

- PSALM 35:13*
  YET WHEN THEY WERE ILL, I PUT ON
  SACKCLOTH AND HUMBLED MYSELF WITH
  FASTING. WHEN MY PRAYERS RETURNED TO
  ME UNANSWERED,
- DEUTERONOMY 8:16*
  HE GAVE YOU MANNA TO EAT IN THE DESERT,
  SOMETHING YOUR FATHERS HAD NEVER
  KNOWN, TO HUMBLE AND TO TEST YOU SO
  THAT IN THE END IT MIGHT GO WELL WITH
  YOU.
- PROVERBS 3:34*
  HE MOCKS PROUD MOCKERS BUT GIVES
  GRACE TO THE HUMBLE.
- 2 CHRONICLES 12:12*
  BECAUSE REHOBOAM HUMBLED HIMSELF,
  THE LORD'S ANGER TURNED FROM HIM, AND
  HE WAS NOT TOTALLY DESTROYED. INDEED,
  THERE WAS SOME GOOD IN JUDAH.

MEDITATE AND ASK JEHOVAH TO OPEN YOUR EYES

JEWS WHO SAY THEY BELIEVE IN JESUS, WHAT IS CENTRAL?

GALATIANS 2:11-21

THE MESSAGE (MSG)

LATER, WHEN PETER CAME TO ANTIOCH(THE FIRST PLACE JESUS BELIEVERS WERE CALLED CHRISTIANS), I HAD A FACE-TO-FACE CONFRONTATION WITH HIM BECAUSE HE WAS CLEARLY OUT OF LINE. HERE'S THE SITUATION. EARLIER, BEFORE CERTAIN PERSONS(JEWISH ELDERS) HAD COME FROM JAMES, PETER REGULARLY ATE WITH THE NON-JEWS(GENTILES). BUT WHEN THAT CONSERVATIVE GROUP(JEWISH ELDERS) CAME FROM JERUSALEM, HE CAUTIOUSLY PULLED BACK AND PUT AS MUCH DISTANCE AS HE COULD MANAGE BETWEEN HIMSELF AND HIS NON-JEWISH(GENTILES) FRIENDS. THAT'S HOW FEARFUL HE WAS OF THE CONSERVATIVE JEWISH CLIQUE(JEWISH ELDERS) THAT'S BEEN PUSHING THE OLD SYSTEM OF CIRCUMCISION. UNFORTUNATELY, THE REST OF THE JEWS IN THE ANTIOCH CHURCH JOINED IN THAT HYPOCRISY SO THAT EVEN BARNABAS WAS SWEPT ALONG IN THE CHARADE.
BUT WHEN I SAW THAT THEY WERE NOT MAINTAINING A STEADY, STRAIGHT COURSE ACCORDING TO THE MESSAGE, I SPOKE UP TO PETER IN FRONT OF THEM ALL: "IF YOU, A JEW, LIVE LIKE A NON-JEW (GENTILES) WHEN YOU'RE NOT BEING

OBSERVED BY THE WATCHDOGS(JEWISH ELDERS) FROM JERUSALEM, WHAT RIGHT DO YOU HAVE TO REQUIRE NON-JEWS(GENTILES) TO CONFORM TO JEWISH CUSTOMS JUST TO MAKE A FAVORABLE IMPRESSION ON YOUR OLD JERUSALEM CRONIES?" WE JEWS KNOW THAT WE HAVE NO ADVANTAGE OF BIRTH OVER "NON-JEWISH SINNERS." WE KNOW VERY WELL THAT WE ARE NOT SET RIGHT WITH GOD BY RULE-KEEPING BUT ONLY THROUGH PERSONAL FAITH IN JESUS CHRIST. HOW DO WE KNOW? WE TRIED IT—AND WE HAD THE BEST SYSTEM OF RULES THE WORLD HAS EVER SEEN! CONVINCED THAT NO HUMAN BEING CAN PLEASE GOD BY SELF-IMPROVEMENT, WE BELIEVED IN JESUS AS THE MESSIAH SO THAT WE MIGHT BE SET RIGHT BEFORE GOD BY TRUSTING IN THE MESSIAH, NOT BY TRYING TO BE GOOD.

HAVE SOME OF YOU NOTICED THAT WE ARE NOT YET PERFECT? (NO GREAT SURPRISE, RIGHT?) AND ARE YOU READY TO MAKE THE ACCUSATION THAT SINCE PEOPLE LIKE ME, WHO GO THROUGH CHRIST IN ORDER TO GET THINGS RIGHT WITH GOD, AREN'T PERFECTLY VIRTUOUS, CHRIST MUST THEREFORE BE AN ACCESSORY TO SIN? THE ACCUSATION IS FRIVOLOUS. IF I WAS "TRYING TO BE GOOD," I WOULD BE REBUILDING THE SAME OLD BARN THAT I TORE DOWN. I WOULD BE ACTING AS A CHARLATAN.

WHAT ACTUALLY TOOK PLACE IS THIS: I TRIED KEEPING RULES AND WORKING MY HEAD OFF TO PLEASE GOD, AND IT DIDN'T WORK. SO I QUIT BEING A "LAW MAN" SO THAT I COULD BE GOD'S MAN. CHRIST'S LIFE SHOWED ME HOW, AND ENABLED ME TO DO IT. I IDENTIFIED MYSELF COMPLETELY WITH HIM.(THIS IS OUR GOAL AS BELIEVERS IN CHRIST) INDEED, I HAVE BEEN CRUCIFIED WITH CHRIST. MY EGO IS NO LONGER CENTRAL(NO PRIDE). IT IS NO LONGER IMPORTANT THAT I APPEAR RIGHTEOUS

BEFORE YOU OR HAVE YOUR GOOD OPINION, AND I AM NO LONGER DRIVEN TO IMPRESS GOD. CHRIST LIVES IN ME. THE LIFE YOU SEE ME LIVING IS NOT "MINE," BUT IT IS LIVED BY FAITH IN THE SON OF GOD, WHO LOVED ME AND GAVE HIMSELF FOR ME. I AM NOT GOING TO GO BACK ON THAT.

IS IT NOT CLEAR TO YOU THAT TO GO BACK TO THAT OLD RULE-KEEPING, PEER-PLEASING RELIGION WOULD BE AN ABANDONMENT OF EVERYTHING PERSONAL AND FREE IN MY RELATIONSHIP WITH GOD? I REFUSE TO DO THAT, TO REPUDIATE GOD'S GRACE. IF A LIVING RELATIONSHIP WITH GOD COULD COME BY RULE-KEEPING, THEN CHRIST DIED UNNECESSARILY.

MEDITATE AND ASK JEHOVAH TO OPEN YOUR EYES

WHY IS JESUS WHITE?

I ASKED THE HOLY SPIRIT,

WHY JESUS WAS ALWAYS PORTRAYED AS A
CAUCASION.

THE HOLY SPIRIT LAUGHED IN MY STOMACH,

AND SAID,

"BLOOD IS EASY TO BE SEEN.

I AM SPIRIT.

WORSHIP ME AS SPIRIT."

JOHN 4:24

GOD IS SPIRIT,
AND

HIS WORSHIPERS MUST WORSHIP IN SPIRIT AND
IN TRUTH."

JOHN 4:23

YET A TIME IS COMING AND HAS NOW COME
WHEN

THE TRUE WORSHIPERS WILL WORSHIP

THE FATHER(JEHOVAH) IN SPIRIT AND TRUTH,

FOR THEY ARE THE KIND OF WORSHIPERS THE
FATHER(JEHOVAH) SEEKS.

MEDITATE AND ASK JEHOVAH TO OPEN YOUR EYES

MOVE YOUR FEAR WITH PSALM 37
A DAVID PSALM

1-2 DON'T BOTHER YOUR HEAD WITH BRAGGARTS
OR WISH YOU COULD SUCCEED LIKE THE WICKED.
IN NO TIME THEY'LL SHRIVEL LIKE GRASS
CLIPPINGS
AND WILT LIKE CUT FLOWERS IN THE SUN.

3-4 GET INSURANCE WITH GOD AND DO A GOOD
DEED,
SETTLE DOWN AND STICK TO YOUR LAST.
KEEP COMPANY WITH GOD,
GET IN ON THE BEST.

5-6 OPEN UP BEFORE GOD, KEEP NOTHING BACK;
HE'LL DO WHATEVER NEEDS TO BE DONE:
HE'LL VALIDATE YOUR LIFE IN THE CLEAR LIGHT
OF DAY
AND STAMP YOU WITH APPROVAL AT HIGH NOON.

7 QUIET DOWN BEFORE GOD,
BE PRAYERFUL BEFORE HIM.
DON'T BOTHER WITH THOSE WHO CLIMB THE
LADDER,
WHO ELBOW THEIR WAY TO THE TOP.

MEDITATE AND ASK JEHOVAH TO OPEN YOUR EYES

8-9 BRIDLE YOUR ANGER, TRASH YOUR WRATH,
COOL YOUR PIPES—IT ONLY MAKES THINGS
WORSE.
BEFORE LONG THE CROOKS WILL BE BANKRUPT;
GOD-INVESTORS WILL SOON OWN THE STORE.

10-11 BEFORE YOU KNOW IT, THE WICKED WILL
HAVE HAD IT;
YOU'LL STARE AT HIS ONCE FAMOUS PLACE
AND—NOTHING!
DOWN-TO-EARTH PEOPLE WILL MOVE IN AND
TAKE OVER,
RELISHING A HUGE BONANZA.

12-13 BAD GUYS HAVE IT IN FOR THE GOOD GUYS,
OBSESSED WITH DOING THEM IN.
BUT GOD ISN'T LOSING ANY SLEEP; TO HIM
THEY'RE A JOKE WITH NO PUNCH LINE.

14-15 BULLIES BRANDISH THEIR SWORDS,
PULL BACK ON THEIR BOWS WITH A FLOURISH.
THEY'RE OUT TO BEAT UP ON THE HARMLESS,
OR MUG THAT NICE MAN OUT WALKING HIS DOG.
A BANANA PEEL LANDS THEM FLAT ON THEIR
FACES—
SLAPSTICK FIGURES IN A MORAL CIRCUS.

MEDITATE AND ASK JEHOVAH TO OPEN YOUR EYES

PSALM 37 CONTINUED

16-17 LESS IS MORE AND MORE IS LESS.
ONE RIGHTEOUS WILL OUTCLASS FIFTY WICKED,
FOR THE WICKED ARE MORAL WEAKLINGS
BUT THE RIGHTEOUS ARE GOD-STRONG.

18-19 GOD KEEPS TRACK OF THE DECENT FOLK;
WHAT THEY DO WON'T SOON BE FORGOTTEN.
IN HARD TIMES, THEY'LL HOLD THEIR HEADS
HIGH;
WHEN THE SHELVES ARE BARE, THEY'LL BE FULL.

20 GOD-DESPISERS HAVE HAD IT;
GOD'S ENEMIES ARE FINISHED—
STRIPPED BARE LIKE VINEYARDS AT HARVEST TIME,
VANISHED LIKE SMOKE IN THIN AIR.

21-22 WICKED BORROWS AND NEVER RETURNS;
RIGHTEOUS GIVES AND GIVES.
GENEROUS GETS IT ALL IN THE END;
STINGY IS CUT OFF AT THE PASS.

MEDITATE AND ASK JEHOVAH TO OPEN YOUR EYES

PSALM 37 CONTINUED

23-24 STALWART WALKS IN STEP WITH GOD;
HIS PATH BLAZED BY GOD, HE'S HAPPY.
IF HE STUMBLES, HE'S NOT DOWN FOR LONG;
GOD HAS A GRIP ON HIS HAND.

25-26 I ONCE WAS YOUNG, NOW I'M A
GRAYBEARD—
NOT ONCE HAVE I SEEN AN ABANDONED
BELIEVER,
OR HIS KIDS OUT ROAMING THE STREETS.
EVERY DAY HE'S OUT GIVING AND LENDING,
HIS CHILDREN MAKING HIM PROUD.

27-28 TURN YOUR BACK ON EVIL,
WORK FOR THE GOOD AND DON'T QUIT.
GOD LOVES THIS KIND OF THING,
NEVER TURNS AWAY FROM HIS FRIENDS.

28-29 LIVE THIS WAY AND YOU'VE GOT IT MADE,
BUT BAD EGGS WILL BE TOSSED OUT.
THE GOOD GET PLANTED ON GOOD LAND
AND PUT DOWN HEALTHY ROOTS.

MEDITATE AND ASK JEHOVAH TO OPEN YOUR EYES

PSALM 37 CONTINUED

30-31 RIGHTEOUS CHEWS ON WISDOM LIKE A
DOG ON A BONE,
ROLLS VIRTUE AROUND ON HIS TONGUE.
HIS HEART PUMPS GOD'S WORD LIKE BLOOD
THROUGH HIS VEINS;
HIS FEET ARE AS SURE AS A CAT'S.

32-33 WICKED SETS A WATCH FOR RIGHTEOUS,
HE'S OUT FOR THE KILL.
GOD, ALERT, IS ALSO ON WATCH—
WICKED WON'T HURT A HAIR OF HIS HEAD.

34 WAIT PASSIONATELY FOR GOD,
DON'T LEAVE THE PATH.
HE'LL GIVE YOU YOUR PLACE IN THE SUN
WHILE YOU WATCH THE WICKED LOSE IT.

35-36 I SAW WICKED BLOATED LIKE A TOAD,
CROAKING PRETENTIOUS NONSENSE.
THE NEXT TIME I LOOKED THERE WAS NOTHING—
A PUNCTURED BLADDER, VAPID AND LIMP.

MEDITATE AND ASK JEHOVAH TO OPEN YOUR EYES

PSALM 37 CONTINUED

37-38 KEEP YOUR EYE ON THE HEALTHY SOUL,
SCRUTINIZE THE STRAIGHT LIFE;
THERE'S A FUTURE
IN STRENUOUS WHOLENESS.
BUT THE WILLFUL WILL SOON BE DISCARDED;
INSOLENT SOULS ARE ON A DEAD-END STREET.

39-40 THE SPACIOUS, FREE LIFE IS FROM GOD,
IT'S ALSO PROTECTED AND SAFE.
GOD-STRENGTHENED, WE'RE DELIVERED FROM
EVIL—
WHEN WE RUN TO HIM, HE SAVES US.

MEDITATE AND ASK JEHOVAH TO OPEN YOUR EYES

PSALM 23

A PSALM OF DAVID.
THE LORD IS MY SHEPHERD, I LACK NOTHING.

HE MAKES ME LIE DOWN IN GREEN PASTURES,
HE LEADS ME BESIDE QUIET WATERS,

HE REFRESHES MY SOUL.
HE GUIDES ME ALONG THE RIGHT PATHS
FOR HIS NAME'S SAKE.

EVEN THOUGH I WALK
THROUGH THE DARKEST VALLEY,
I WILL FEAR NO EVIL,
FOR YOU ARE WITH ME;
YOUR ROD AND YOUR STAFF,
THEY COMFORT ME.
YOU PREPARE A TABLE BEFORE ME
IN THE PRESENCE OF MY ENEMIES.
YOU ANOINT MY HEAD WITH OIL;
MY CUP OVERFLOWS.

SURELY YOUR GOODNESS AND LOVE WILL FOLLOW
ME
ALL THE DAYS OF MY LIFE,
AND I WILL DWELL IN THE HOUSE OF THE LORD
FOREVER.

MEDITATE AND ASK JEHOVAH TO OPEN YOUR EYES

PSALM 103

OF DAVID.
1 PRAISE THE LORD, O MY SOUL;
ALL MY INMOST BEING, PRAISE HIS HOLY NAME.
2 PRAISE THE LORD, O MY SOUL,
AND FORGET NOT ALL HIS BENEFITS—
3 WHO FORGIVES ALL YOUR SINS
AND HEALS ALL YOUR DISEASES,
4 WHO REDEEMS YOUR LIFE FROM THE PIT
AND CROWNS YOU WITH LOVE AND
COMPASSION,
5 WHO SATISFIES YOUR DESIRES WITH GOOD
THINGS
SO THAT YOUR YOUTH IS RENEWED LIKE THE
EAGLE'S.
6 THE LORD WORKS RIGHTEOUSNESS
AND JUSTICE FOR ALL THE OPPRESSED.
7 HE MADE KNOWN HIS WAYS TO MOSES,
HIS DEEDS TO THE PEOPLE OF ISRAEL:
8 THE LORD IS COMPASSIONATE AND GRACIOUS,
SLOW TO ANGER, ABOUNDING IN LOVE.
9 HE WILL NOT ALWAYS ACCUSE,
NOR WILL HE HARBOR HIS ANGER FOREVER;
10 HE DOES NOT TREAT US AS OUR SINS DESERVE
OR REPAY US ACCORDING TO OUR INIQUITIES.
11 FOR AS HIGH AS THE HEAVENS ARE ABOVE THE
EARTH,
SO GREAT IS HIS LOVE FOR THOSE WHO FEAR HIM;
12 AS FAR AS THE EAST IS FROM THE WEST,
SO FAR HAS HE REMOVED OUR TRANSGRESSIONS
FROM US.

13 AS A FATHER HAS COMPASSION ON HIS
CHILDREN,
SO THE LORD HAS COMPASSION ON THOSE WHO
FEAR HIM;
14 FOR HE KNOWS HOW WE ARE FORMED,
HE REMEMBERS THAT WE ARE DUST.
15 AS FOR MAN, HIS DAYS ARE LIKE GRASS,
HE FLOURISHES LIKE A FLOWER OF THE FIELD;
16 THE WIND BLOWS OVER IT AND IT IS GONE,
AND ITS PLACE REMEMBERS IT NO MORE.
17 BUT FROM EVERLASTING TO EVERLASTING
THE LORD'S LOVE IS WITH THOSE WHO FEAR HIM,
AND HIS RIGHTEOUSNESS WITH THEIR
CHILDREN'S CHILDREN—
18 WITH THOSE WHO KEEP HIS COVENANT
AND REMEMBER TO OBEY HIS PRECEPTS.
19 THE LORD HAS ESTABLISHED HIS THRONE IN
HEAVEN,
AND HIS KINGDOM RULES OVER ALL.
20 PRAISE THE LORD, YOU HIS ANGELS,
YOU MIGHTY ONES WHO DO HIS BIDDING,
WHO OBEY HIS WORD.
21 PRAISE THE LORD, ALL HIS HEAVENLY HOSTS,
YOU HIS SERVANTS WHO DO HIS WILL.
22 PRAISE THE LORD, ALL HIS WORKS
EVERYWHERE IN HIS DOMINION.
PRAISE THE LORD, O MY SOUL.

MEDITATE AND ASK JEHOVAH TO OPEN YOUR EYES

WHEN WE GO AGAINST GOD'S PROPHETS IT WILL COST US.

JEREMIAH 20
JEREMIAH AND PASHHUR(PASTORS AND RABBIS)

WHEN THE PRIEST PASHHUR SON OF IMMER, THE CHIEF OFFICER IN THE TEMPLE OF THE LORD, HEARD JEREMIAH PROPHESYING THESE THINGS, 2 HE HAD JEREMIAH THE PROPHET BEATEN AND PUT IN THE STOCKS AT THE UPPER GATE OF BENJAMIN AT THE LORD'S TEMPLE. 3 THE NEXT DAY, WHEN PASHHUR RELEASED HIM FROM THE STOCKS, JEREMIAH SAID TO HIM, "THE LORD'S NAME FOR YOU IS NOT PASHHUR, BUT MAGOR-MISSABIB. 4 FOR THIS IS WHAT THE LORD SAYS: 'I WILL MAKE YOU A TERROR TO YOURSELF AND TO ALL YOUR FRIENDS; WITH YOUR OWN EYES YOU WILL SEE THEM FALL BY THE SWORD OF THEIR ENEMIES. I WILL HAND ALL JUDAH OVER TO THE KING OF BABYLON, WHO WILL CARRY THEM AWAY TO BABYLON OR PUT THEM TO THE SWORD. 5 I WILL HAND OVER TO THEIR ENEMIES ALL THE WEALTH OF THIS CITY—ALL ITS PRODUCTS, ALL ITS VALUABLES AND ALL THE TREASURES OF THE KINGS OF JUDAH. THEY WILL TAKE IT AWAY AS PLUNDER AND CARRY IT OFF TO BABYLON. 6 AND YOU, PASHHUR, AND ALL WHO LIVE IN YOUR HOUSE WILL GO INTO EXILE TO BABYLON. THERE YOU WILL DIE AND BE BURIED, YOU AND ALL YOUR FRIENDS TO WHOM YOU HAVE PROPHESIED LIES.'"

MEDITATE AND ASK JEHOVAH TO OPEN YOUR EYES

GOD THOUGHTS

ISAIAH 55:8-11

FOR MY THOUGHTS ARE NOT YOUR THOUGHTS,
NEITHER ARE YOUR WAYS MY WAYS,"
DECLARES THE LORD.
AS THE HEAVENS ARE HIGHER THAN THE EARTH,
SO ARE MY WAYS HIGHER THAN YOUR WAYS
AND MY THOUGHTS THAN YOUR THOUGHTS.
AS THE RAIN AND THE SNOW
COME DOWN FROM HEAVEN,
AND DO NOT RETURN TO IT
WITHOUT WATERING THE EARTH
AND MAKING IT BUD AND FLOURISH,
SO THAT IT YIELDS SEED FOR THE SOWER AND
BREAD FOR THE EATER,
SO IS MY WORD THAT GOES OUT FROM MY
MOUTH:
IT WILL NOT RETURN TO ME EMPTY,
BUT WILL ACCOMPLISH WHAT I DESIRE
AND ACHIEVE THE PURPOSE FOR WHICH I SENT IT.

MEDITATE AND ASK JEHOVAH TO OPEN YOUR EYES

EVERY HUMAN SHOULD HAVE ACCESS TO A PROPHET.

DON'T LET SATAN STOP YOU FROM FINDING A
PROPHET.

BECAUSE SATAN KNOWS SCRIPTURE,
HE KNOWS THAT GOD'S
MOST DIRECT WAY TO
COMMUNICATE TO HUMANS
IS THROUGH HIS PROPHETS.
HENCE, HE HAS MADE MOST HUMANS
AVOID PROPHETS BASED ON CHARACTER
ASSASSINATION AND PROPAGANDA.

AMOS 3:7

SURELY THE SOVEREIGN LORD DOES NOTHING
WITHOUT REVEALING HIS PLAN
TO HIS SERVANTS THE PROPHETS.

1 CORINTHIANS 14
GIFTS OF PROPHECY AND TONGUES

1 FOLLOW THE WAY OF LOVE AND EAGERLY DESIRE
SPIRITUAL GIFTS,
ESPECIALLY THE GIFT OF PROPHECY.
2 FOR ANYONE WHO SPEAKS IN A TONGUE DOES
NOT SPEAK TO MEN BUT TO GOD.

INDEED, NO ONE UNDERSTANDS HIM;
HE UTTERS MYSTERIES WITH HIS SPIRIT.
3 BUT EVERYONE WHO PROPHESIES SPEAKS TO
MEN FOR THEIR STRENGTHENING,
ENCOURAGEMENT AND COMFORT.

MEDITATE AND ASK JEHOVAH TO OPEN YOUR EYES

HEAR, O ISRAEL: THE LORD OUR GOD, THE LORD IS ONE.

DEUTERONOMY 6:4

JOHN 14:12-14

VERY TRULY I TELL YOU,
WHOEVER BELIEVES IN ME
WILL DO THE WORKS I HAVE BEEN DOING,
AND
THEY WILL DO EVEN GREATER THINGS THAN
THESE,
BECAUSE I AM GOING TO THE FATHER.
AND
I WILL DO WHATEVER YOU ASK IN MY NAME,
SO THAT THE FATHER MAY BE GLORIFIED IN THE
SON.
YOU MAY ASK ME FOR ANYTHING IN MY NAME,
AND
I WILL DO IT.

JOHN 15:7

IF YOU REMAIN IN ME
AND
MY WORDS REMAIN IN YOU,
ASK WHATEVER YOU WISH,
AND
IT WILL BE DONE FOR YOU.

MEDITATE AND ASK JEHOVAH TO OPEN YOUR EYES

THE CRITERIA FOR CHILDLIKE FAITH IN GOD

DEUTERONOMY 6:4

HEAR, O ISRAEL: THE LORD OUR GOD, THE LORD IS ONE.

BY SURPRISE SITHOLE

JESUS GAVE THE CRITERIA TO HIM

DO NOT CRITICIZE ANYONE ANYTIME

DO NOT ARGUE WITH ANYONE ANYTIME

LOVE AND RESPECT EVERYONE

STAY HAPPY AND THANKFUL ALWAYS

MEDITATE AND ASK JEHOVAH TO OPEN YOUR EYES

ALL PALISTINIANS WILL DIE

OBADIAH 1:15

THE MESSAGE (MSG)
15-18 "GOD'S JUDGMENT DAY IS NEAR
FOR ALL THE GODLESS NATIONS.
AS YOU HAVE DONE, IT WILL BE DONE TO YOU.
WHAT YOU DID WILL BOOMERANG BACK
AND HIT YOUR OWN HEAD.
JUST AS YOU PARTIED ON MY HOLY MOUNTAIN,
ALL THE GODLESS NATIONS WILL DRINK GOD'S
WRATH.
THEY'LL DRINK AND DRINK AND DRINK—
THEY'LL DRINK THEMSELVES TO DEATH.
BUT NOT SO ON MOUNT ZION—THERE'S RESPITE
THERE!
A SAFE AND HOLY PLACE!
THE FAMILY OF JACOB WILL TAKE BACK THEIR
POSSESSIONS
FROM THOSE WHO TOOK THEM FROM THEM.
THAT'S WHEN THE FAMILY OF JACOB WILL CATCH
FIRE,
THE FAMILY OF JOSEPH BECOME FIERCE FLAME,
WHILE THE FAMILY OF ESAU WILL BE STRAW.
ESAU WILL GO UP IN FLAMES,
NOTHING LEFT OF ESAU BUT A PILE OF ASHES."
GOD SAID IT, AND IT IS SO.